# THE SNEAKER BOOK

## 50 Years of Sports Shoe Design

Melissa Cardona

4880 Lower Valley Road, Atglen, PA 19310 USA

# Acknowledgments

Many thanks go to West Chester University and the staff of the Francis Harvey Green Library, especially to Nancy, Walter, and Sally, for sharing their resources and workspace with me.

Library of Congress Cataloging-in-Publication Data
Cardona, Melissa.
  The sneaker book : 50 years of sport shoe design / by Melissa Cardona.
     p. cm.
  ISBN 0-7643-2188-9 (hardcover)
1. Sneakers—Pictorial works. 2. Athletic shoes—Pictorial works. I. Title.

GV749.S64C37 2005
685'.31—dc22

2005002316

Covers and book designed by Bruce Waters
Type set in Futura X-Bold heading font/text font Times Roman

ISBN: 0-7643-2188-9
Printed in China

Published by Schiffer Publishing Ltd.
4880 Lower Valley Road
Atglen, PA 19310
Phone: (610) 593-1777; Fax: (610) 593-2002
E-mail: Info@schifferbooks.com

For the largest selection of fine reference books on this and related subjects, please visit our web site at **www.schifferbooks.com**
We are always looking for people to write books on new and related subjects. If you have an idea for a book please contact us at the above address.

This book may be purchased from the publisher.
Include $3.95 for shipping.
Please try your bookstore first.
You may write for a free catalog.

In Europe, Schiffer books are distributed by
Bushwood Books
6 Marksbury Ave.
Kew Gardens
Surrey TW9 4JF England
Phone: 44 (0) 20 8392-8585; Fax: 44 (0) 20 8392-9876
E-mail: info@bushwoodbooks.co.uk
Free postage in the U.K., Europe; air mail at cost.

# Contents

## Author's Note

The photographs in this book feature images in magazine advertisements from the 1940s through the 1980s. The information presented in *The Sneaker Book* is based on text included in original advertisements. Names of manufacturers, shoe styles, and technologies may be trademarked, and they are used in this book as an historical record to describe the shoes with the same nomenclature used by the manufacturers.

To Chris...because he loves sneakers,
and I love him.

# Introduction

What do rubber manufacturers, celebrity athletes, podiatrists, and urban youth all have in common? Though seemingly disparate groups, they have all been instrumental in the spawning of one of the twentieth century's most iconic items: the sneaker. The history of athletic shoes is the stuff that myths are made of – filled with legendary characters, gold medal victories, and enormous profit-making potential. Perhaps more than any other manufactured product, the sneaker truly embodies the spirit of the twentieth century – its emphasis on technology, mass media marketing, corporate profit making, and an increasingly global economy.

The story of athletic footwear is stitched together by a series of technological innovations that revolutionized not only the way that sneakers were designed and manufactured, but also the marketing strategies used to promote them. This history probably begins somewhere in the mid- to late nineteenth century, when Charles Goodyear accidentally spilled a combination of sulfur and rubber on a hot surface, thereby discovering the vulcanization process. Vulcanization allowed rubber and cloth to be molded together, and was used by the Goodyear company to develop the patented Goodyear Welt. The basis for modern sports shoe designs, vulcanization replaced the less durable method of stitching a rubber sole and cloth or leather upper together.

From then on, countless patents were issued to sneaker manufacturers for innovative technologies, all designed to improve athletic performance. A proliferation of unique arch supports, special soles, heel tabs, and hi-tech inserts were the results of scientific research and exhaustive studies performed to better understand the needs and problems of athletes' feet. As the market for athletic footwear expanded, manufacturers began producing increasingly specialized shoes for individual sports, using these unique features as selling points in their advertising.

Although sneaker companies employed science and gimmicky features to design and market their products throughout the twentieth century, it wasn't until the 1970s that science really became the backbone of sneaker design. Podiatrists began participating in the development of corrective devices in athletic footwear, fueled by a growing understanding of and interest in biomechanics, and a flourishing health craze. These technological innovations and studies significantly propelled the cost of sneakers upward, nonetheless, the athletic footwear industry boomed in the '70s.

During the 1980s, the athletic shoe industry experienced yet another transformation and increase in profits – stimulated heavily by the fashion- and status-conscious tastes of urban youth, and the subsequent proliferation of sneakers off the court. As the popularity of sneakers as leisurewear grew, sneaker manufacturers began producing increasingly outrageous and complex athletic shoe designs, a trend that continues today despite the high cost of these products. Each year, millions of dollars are poured into biomechanical engineering and research, but fashion largely dictates what sells in the athletic footwear industry.

One of the latest trends to dominate the sneaker industry is the growing demand for vintage sneakers. These classic designs are highly coveted and traded on e-bay and in vintage shops, and have even been re-issued by their manufacturers. While complex and super hi-tech sneakers still represent the future of athletic shoe design, there is an interest in the simpler models of the past.

This book is filled with simple, classic designs, as well as some early predecessors of today's hi-tech shoes. It is intended to trace the development of sports shoe design from the 1940s through the 1980s, providing a historical record of sneaker models advertised in athletic magazines during that period. The text written to accompany the images is based on information included in the advertisements, and is intended to reflect the marketing strategies used to promote the products featured. It is the hope of the author that this historical record of athletic shoe design provides insight into the transformation and growth of the industry, as well as helps readers draw their own conclusions about the role of the sneaker as an icon of the twentieth century.

These leather basketball shoes from Riddell were touted as the "fastest starting and stopping shoes on the market." They came in black uppers with black or non-marking soles, or a dressier white upper with non-marking soles.

The Converse 6-Man Football Shoe featured semi-rigid rubber cleats, reinforced box toes, sponge cushion heels, and arch support. This canvas shoe cost two-thirds less than its leather counterparts, but offered the same support to field sports athletes.

8

THIS IS THE SHOE YOU'LL WANT!

CONVERSE
RUBBER COMPANY
MALDEN, MASSACHUSETTS

CHICAGO: 212 W. Monroe St.    ST. PAUL: 242 E. 5th St.    NEW YORK: 200 Church St.

1  BLACK CANVAS "ALL STAR" . . .
   Continues to outsell any basketball
   shoe made.

2  BLACK LEATHER "ALL STAR" . . .
   Entirely new "All Star" of yellow-
   back "Kanga" leather with new welt
   type outsole construction.

3  LEATHER "COURT STAR" . . .
   Newly styled blue-back "Kanga"
   leather basketball shoe with improved
   construction features.

CONVERSE BASKETBALL YEAR BOOK
for 1938-1939 season now ready. 44 pages,
over 300 teams, articles of value to every
coach and player. Send for your FREE COPY.

# CONVERSE

*"Chuck" Taylor*

# ALL STARS

9

*Converse. The Athletic Journal, Oct. 1939*

**"Chuck" Taylor All-Stars from Converse. These famous, best-
selling basketball shoes were originally available in black only.**

# BLACK CANVAS "ALL STAR"

YOU and your players will go big, but big, for the dramatic black-and-white smartness of this new 1948 model "All Star." It's a natural for tournament play.

"Chucks" were advertised as lightweight basketball shoes with double strength toe guards, extra cushion insoles with arch support, high peg tops for ankle support, reinforced eyelets, and non-marking molded outsoles that provided traction on any floor.

10

# WHITE OLYMPIC "ALL STAR"

This striking white canvas "All Star," with its red, white and blue motif, reflects national interest in the forthcoming Olympic Games. This is a white shoe — *plus!*

**12**

This 1942 advertisement from Converse called on coaches and athletes to take care of their basketball shoes, as changes in production during WWII meant supplies were scarce.

MR. COACH...
MR. ATHLETIC DIRECTOR...
MR. TEAM MANAGER...
MR. BASKETBALL PLAYER...

War times demand that you
# TAKE CARE of your Basketball Shoes...

*GET extra seasons' service from your present Converse Basketball Shoes by following these sensible precautions*

**T**HE SUPPLY of Converse basketball shoes for the 1942-43 season will be limited. Dealers' stocks won't be anywhere large enough to fill next season's demands for basketball's most popular footwear. BUT . . . there's plenty of EXTRA WEAR still remaining in a large percentage of the shoes used this past season. IF you'll follow the common-sense suggestions outlined here for their proper care. Sensible care NOW assures satisfactory wear LATER. Help maintain the speed and fire and flash of America's greatest sport — take proper care of your Converse basketball shoes!

## BETWEEN-SEASON CARE OF CONVERSE SHOES

(1) Wash thoroughly inside and out with MILD soap-and-water solution.

(2) Allow to dry thoroughly at NORMAL room temperatures—NEVER near radiators, stove or in strong sunlight.

(3) Have shoemaker repair any breaks or tears in uppers.

(4) Lace loosely and stuff to top with tissue paper.

(5) Store in cool, dark, dry place.

### SPECIAL WARNING

*Don't use hard-to-replace basketball shoes for ordinary outdoor wear . . . save them for basketball!*

# CONVERSE
## RUBBER COMPANY
### MALDEN, MASSACHUSETTS

CHICAGO: 212 W. Monroe Street
ST. PAUL: 242 E. Fifth Street
NEW YORK: 200 Church Street

*for* APRIL, 1942

11

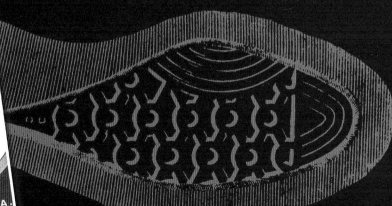

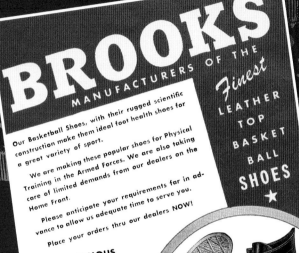

# BROOKS

### MANUFACTURERS OF THE

*Finest*

LEATHER
TOP
BASKET
BALL
SHOES
★

Our Basketball Shoes, with their rugged scientific construction make them ideal foot health shoes for a great variety of sport.

We are making these popular shoes for Physical Training in the Armed Forces. We are also taking care of limited demands from our dealers on the Home Front.

Please anticipate your requirements far in advance to allow us adequate time to serve you.

Place your orders thru our dealers NOW!

OTHER FAMOUS
## BROOKS SHOES
FOR
BASEBALL
SOFTBALL
FOOTBALL
BOWLING
PHYSICAL TRAINING
BOXING-WRESTLING
TRACK        SOCCER
LACROSSE

# BROOKS
SHOE MFG. CO.
58TH AND MARKET STS. PHILADELPHIA PA.

In 1944, Brooks advertised their production of shoes for physical training in the armed forces. The company boasted a "rugged scientific construction" that made the shoes ideal for many sports.

A.G. Spalding & Bros., *The Athletic Journal*, Dec. 1939

14

Spalding's SS Basketball Shoes were said to give "split-second foot control," and came with red rubber soles, army duck uppers, and white rubber toe bumpers.

Spot-Bilt's leather basketball shoes featured stitching on the non-skid soles and heels cushioned with sponge rubber. "Numbering Cards" could be inserted into the shoes' "Spot Pocket," which was useful to a team's equipment man for easy identification.

Spot-Bilt, *The Athletic Journal*, Oct. 1939

Wilson Sporting Goods Co., *The Athletic Journal*, Oct. 1939

Wilson advertised their basketball uniforms as "inspiring," and ensured coaches that their players were sure to play inspired basketball in them. This advertisement stated that showmanship was a vital part of the modern basketball game, and the new uniform styles from Wilson were an essential element. The uniforms were available in any color combinations.

16

The Cager, Comet, and Big Leaguer basketball shoes from Keds included a "Scientific Last" system with straight-line toe action and even weight distribution. The shoes also featured shock-proof insoles and flexible arch cushions.

YOUR BOYS KNOW TIME FOR ACTION IS

TIME FOR **Keds** REG. U. S. PAT. OFF.

BIG LEAGUER

COMET

CAGER

FOR BASKETBALL AND GYMNASIUM WEAR

Keds/The United States Rubber Company, *The Athletic Journal*, Sept. 1939

The Epler football shoe by Keds was "developed by the man who originated the game." Stephen Epler was a high school coach in Nebraska during the depression who created the game of six-man football for his small school, which didn't have enough players for 11-man football. Also looking for ways to save money, he developed a soft-soled shoe, which was cheaper than shoes with cleats. This shoe, with a felt-padded tongue, special kicking toe, and slant-cut top were promoted as ideal features for football players.

The Comet for basketball and Majestic Oxford for tennis by Keds.

Keds/The United States Rubber Company, *The Athletic Journal*, Jan. 1940

17

Keds/The United States Rubber Company, *The Athletic Journal*, Mar. 1940

SPEED with SAFETY and COMFORT..

The *Official*

SHOE

HELPS WIN GAMES

The OFFICIAL is also made all-white with a black edging on the sole binding strip.

Ball-Band Mishawaka Rubber & Mfg. Co. advertisement, October 1939

The Ball-Band Official's ventilated cushion insole was designed to keep a player's feet cool. A system of channels and holes in the insoles acted as "air conditioning."

The Hoopster was advertised as a vulcanized shoe, with the sole and upper forming one complete unit. The reinforced upper had two plies of heavy duck, a peg top, and a tape cloth back stay. Four plies of fabric were used over the vamp to prevent ripping due to flexing of the foot.

20

## "THE BUY OF THE YEAR"

### THE HOOD "HOOPSTER"
#### with new "RUBALOCK" SOLE

This new sole is built on the principle of modern non-skid tires, with 4 levels and "staggered" tread. Positive grip on any type of floor for quick stops and pivots.

Hood Athletic Footwear, *The Athletic Journal*, Sept. 1939

RUBALOCK SOLE

P.F.*

*Posture Foundation

INSIDE WEDGE ARCH SUPPORT

**21**

Hood basketball shoes came equipped with the scientifically developed P.F., or Posture Foundation, to help keep feet in a normal position and prevent flat feet and leg fatigue. The shoes' special design also featured the non-skid "Rubalock" sole, designed to mimic non-skid tires with four levels of staggered tread.

**THE HOOPSTER —**
Again the "Buy of the Year" has "Rubalock" sole, "P.F.," vulcanized process construction, Hygeen cushion insole, sponge cushion heel, four-ply vamp, smooth inside, ventilated extra quality canvas uppers.

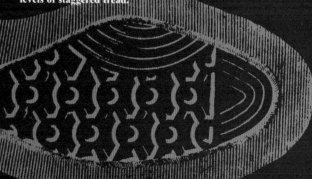

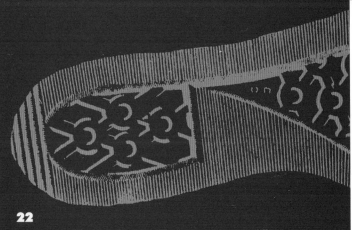

22

Beacon Falls Rubber Footwear advertised their Flash basketball shoes as "the pioneer of all modern basketball shoe improvements." The list of features included a moulded double heel cushion, "snugfit arch," and long-wearing outsole with proper traction. They were available in white and black, and in men's and women's sizes.

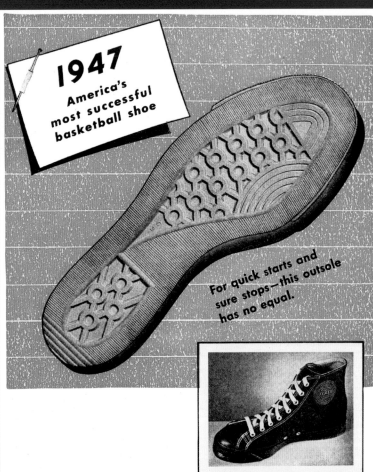

**1947**

America's most successful basketball shoe

For quick starts and sure stops—this outsole has no equal.

Beacon Falls Rubber Footwear, The Athletic Journal, Sept. 1947

Beacon Falls Rubber Footwear in The Official Journal, Sept. 1949

# TOP NOTCH-50 YEARS NEW

This year marks the Fiftieth Anniversary for the makers of the famous Top Notch basketball footwear. And we can truthfully say that Top Notch is 50 years new because nearly every year, starting with the famed 1914 Gripsure molded outsole, Top Notch has introduced *new designs* and *new features* for the foot comfort and foot protection of your players!

## INTRODUCING...

New color combinations in the Collegiate

Double heel cushion
Eliminates bone
bruises

Built up arch cushion
fast action comfort

Full cushion insole
Complete foot
protection

SPONGE HEEL

SNUGFIT ARCH

**TOP NOTCH**

**BEACON FALLS RUBBER FOOTWEAR**
BEACON FALLS CONNECTICUT

**COACHES**
Place your 1949 orders now with your Sporting Goods Dealers!

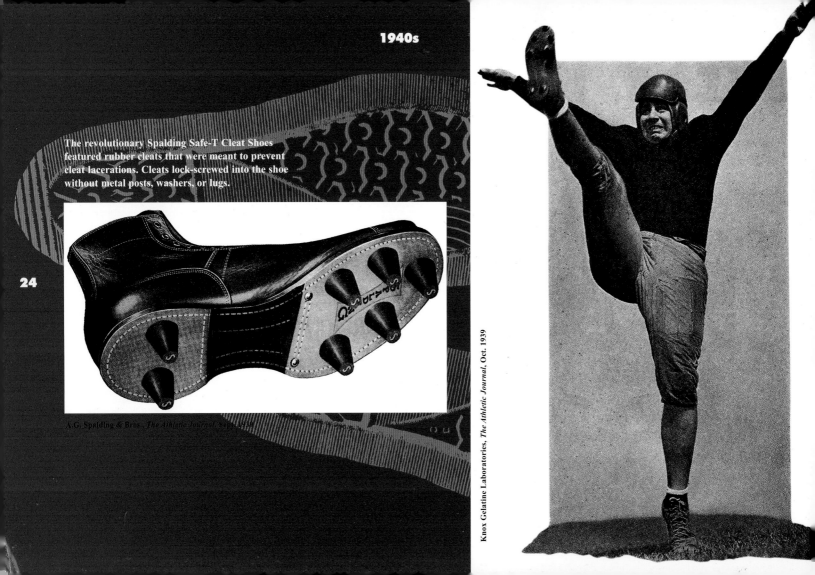

The revolutionary Spalding Safe-T Cleat Shoes featured rubber cleats that were meant to prevent cleat lacerations. Cleats lock-screwed into the shoe without metal posts, washers, or lugs.

24

A.G. Spalding & Bros., *The Athletic Journal, Sept. 1939*

Knox Gelatine Laboratories, *The Athletic Journal*, Oct. 1939

It won't happen with BROOKS . . .

# ONLY FOOTBALL SHOES with the CLEATS THAT CAN'T COME OFF!

Patented "Lock-Tite" Washers and Ratchet Nuts, exclusive with Brooks, help you to build a winning team from the ground up . . . in three ways!

**SAFETY** . . . Outer row of ratchets on washer interlocks firmly with cleat . . . injury-making bolts are never exposed!

**SPEED** . . . Inner row of ratchets interlocks with ratchet nut . . . the bolt can't "back up" to cause handicapping blisters!

**LONGER WEAR** . . . Cleat assembly holds firm for the life of the shoe . . . shoes need not be discarded because of loose bolts!

Available in
Collegiate, Professional
and High School
Models

## BROOKS
### SHOE MANUFACTURING CO.
PHILADELPHIA 39, PA.

Brooks Shoe Manufacturing Co., *The Athletic Journal*, Oct. 1947

Paxr shoes by Spalding were made with yellow-back kangaroo uppers, Goodyear construction, sole-leather counters, box toes, and semi-flexible sprint shanks.

A.G. Spalding & Bros., *The Athletic Journal*, Apr. 1948

John T. Riddell, Inc., *The Athletic Journal*, Jan. 1940

**These Riddell track and field shoes featured interchangeable spikes that came in three lengths.**

Wilson's Famous Player baseball shoes featured yellow-back Kangaroo uppers with Goodyear welt. The hand-forged steel spikes were positioned in relation to the foot bones for maximum power and minimal muscle strain.

Wilson Sporting Goods Co., *The Athletic Journal*, Mar. 1948

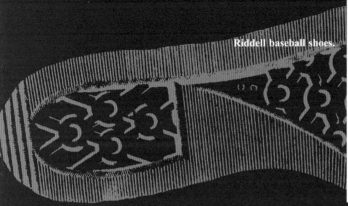

Riddell baseball shoes.

John T. Riddell, Inc., *The Athletic Journal*, Jan. 1940

28

The Model 720 R from Spot-Bilt, a kangaroo leather warm-up or cross country shoe in blue-black. Light and flexible, the shoe featured a straight foam rubber sole and was made with non-stretch nylon reinforcements. Also available in athletic tanned cowhide.

Baseball shoes from Spot-Bilt, with a sponge rubber sock lining and scientifically designed lasts to provide perfect balance. Available in yellowback or blueback kangaroo uppers.

30

Post Manufacturing Co., Inc., *The Athletic Journal*, Oct. 1957

Spot-Bilt, *The Athletic Journal*, Sept. 1953

Spot-Bilt's kangaroo football shoes with double stitched flexible shank, straight in the soles and soft in the toes.

Kangaroo leather track shoes from Spot-Bilt with special chrome tanned leather sole and heal lift for long wear.

Spot-Bilt, *The Athletic Journal*, Sept. 1953

Spot-Bilt, *The Athletic Journal*, Sept. 1953

31

The T 22 sprint track shoe from Spalding was reinforced with a strip of white elk to help prevent stretching. Tempered steel outdoor spikes were detachable.

Spalding, *The Athletic Journal*, Nov. 1953

More Spalding track shoes. From left: 11 TR-2 with Goodyear lock-stitching; the 114 Indoor/Outdoor shoe; and the T 26 with natural oak leather taps.

Spalding, *The Athletic Journal*, Nov. 1953

Converse Rubber Company, *The Athletic Journal*, Nov. 1957

PINPOINT DESIGN
MOLDED SOLE

Assuring better footwork and maximum comfort
COURT STAR (laca-to-toe)
NET KING (circular vamp)

MEN'S
4 to 14
WOS.
4 to 10

CUSHION
HEEL

Your choice
of two
positive-traction
soles

NON-SKID
MOLDED SOLE

Sure traction on wet surfaces,
grass or polished playing courts
SLIPNOT (laca-to-toe and circular vamp models)

CUSHION
HEEL

MEN'S
4 to 14
WOS.
4 to 9

These Converse tennis shoes were designed to provide traction on the court.

The Racer and Track Star from Converse featured crepe rubber soles and heels.

33

Converse Rubber Company, *The Athletic Journal*, Nov. 1957

"Caterpillar tread soles" on 'Pro' Keds basketball shoes were advertised as giving players more control and speed on the court.

**34**

THE CHOICE OF EXPERIENCED COACHES

THE **COLLEGIATE**

Exclusive Side Lang Lacing relieves instep strain . . . creates added ankle support. Other comfort features you know. Top Notch basketball shoes mean protection for your players.

Top College and Pro teams will be wearing new, color combination Collegiates this season. Top coaches know Top Notch basketball shoes mean protection for your players.

**BEACON FALLS RUBBER FOOTWEAR**
BEACON FALLS, CONNECTICUT

*Beacon Falls Rubber Footwear, The Athletic Journal, Mar. 1950*

Double heel cushion, to prevent painful bruises. Extra protection at arch.

White, Black, Blue, Red, Gold. Team color laces also available.

Pull-up side stays with extra reinforcing piece.

New, special rubber compound with extra cling, toughness.

Uppers are lightweight, loose lined, have breathe holes.

Block action tread soles grip in all directions.

Pivot pad is extra large, flat for speed-turns.

Tempered toe bumper for extra wear.

*U.S. Keds/U.S. Rubber Co., The Athletic Journal, Sept. 1953*

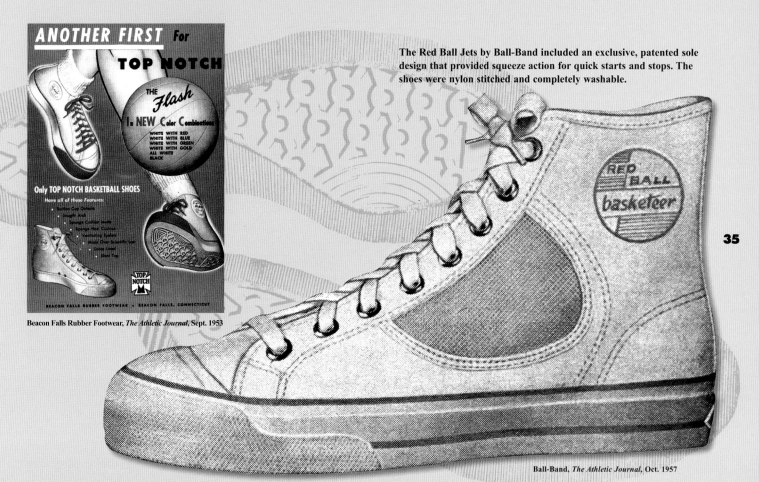

ANOTHER FIRST For
TOP NOTCH

THE *Flash*
In NEW Color Combinations
WHITE WITH RED
WHITE WITH BLUE
WHITE WITH GREEN
WHITE WITH GOLD
ALL WHITE
BLACK

Only TOP NOTCH BASKETBALL SHOES
*Have all of these Features:*

BEACON FALLS RUBBER FOOTWEAR • BEACON FALLS, CONNECTICUT

Beacon Falls Rubber Footwear, *The Athletic Journal*, Sept. 1953

The Red Ball Jets by Ball-Band included an exclusive, patented sole design that provided squeeze action for quick starts and stops. The shoes were nylon stitched and completely washable.

RED BALL basketeer

35

Ball-Band, *The Athletic Journal*, Oct. 1957

Wilson, *The Athletic Journal*, Oct. 1957

Wilson, *The Athletic Journal*, Oct. 1957

# Trying to improve their game?

## Improve their shoe!

Pro-Keds/U.S. Rubber, *The Athletic Journal*, May 1962

Pedigree
Field event shoe of unmatched balance, stability. Outer edge, left shoe has Wrap-around neoprene sole to reduce outer edge rolling and knee strain.

TRACKSTER
Famous "RIPPLE" Sole
Bantam Rib
Reduces fatigue
Lengthens the stride
Improves traction
Prevents stone bruises
Helps prevent "shin splints"

Ask about our "ON APPROVAL" offer to Coaches
Write

New Balance, *The Athletic Journal*, Nov. 1961

Pro-Keds U.S. Rubber, *The Athletic Journal*, May 1962

The U.S. Royal Pro-Keds basketball shoe was advertised as the "first major break-through in years of basketball shoes." The shoes made their debut in 1959.

Keds' Royal Oxfords were designed with a "stay-on strap" to prevent the shoes from accidentally slipping off or causing blisters. A "revolutionary new compound so remarkably durable" was used for the shoes' soles.

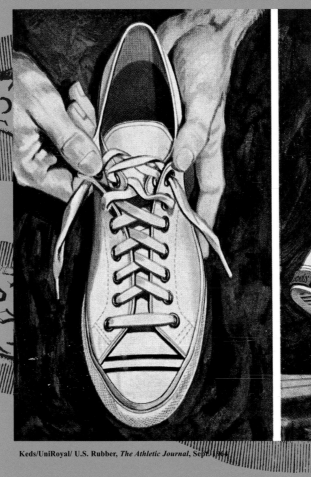
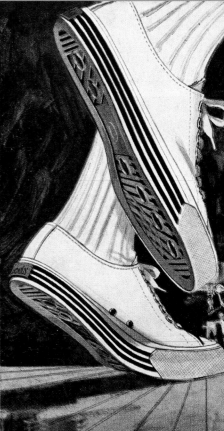

Keds/UniRoyal/ U.S. Rubber, *The Athletic Journal*, Sept. 1964

**F9114.** Finest blue-back Kangaroo available in high-cut. Rugged construction with leather outsole. Detachable polyurethane cleats.

**F9124.** Deluxe model with genuine blue-back Kangaroo leather featuring new idea in cleat placement—six cleats in front instead five.

**F9042.** Strap-Lock oxford in combination blue-back kangaroo and horsehide. Polyurethane cleats. Also available as high-cut.

**F9032.** Wing-tip styling in quality blue-back kangaroo. Drilite outsole. Detachable cleats. Also available as high-cut.

**F9144.** New shoe with six-cleats in forepart, molded into the polyurethane outsole. Athletic cowhide uppers. Also low-cut oxford.

Football shoes from Wilson.

**41**

**F9160.** Moderately priced shoe with specially tanned blue-back athletic cowhide uppers, detachable nylon cleats.

**F9000.** Coaches' and trainers' shoe of quality blue-back kangaroo with Ripple rubber outsole.

**F9052.** Blue-back athletic cowhide shoe with Strap-Lock feature that pulls heel section up snugly. Traditional high-cut shoe also available.

These track shoes from Wilson introduced a wider area for the balls of the feet, foam-cushioned tongues, and padded toes.

PLAY TO WIN WITH

**Wilson**

Wilson Sporting Goods Co., Chicago
(A subsidiary of Wilson & Co., Inc.)

WILSON STRAP-LOCK holds shoe snugly in place. Blue-back kangaroo. Six spikes.

WILSON FIELD EVENTS SHOE. Blue-back kangaroo. Six spikes in sole and one in heel.

K6806 / K6836 / K6866

Wilson, *The Athletic Journal*, January 1962.

Magnus soccer shoes with a flexible cushion collar made from kangaroo leather.

**SOCCER-FOOTBALL**

CAN BE RESOLED. Cushion flex collar. Made on football lasts with football patterns. Multi studded sole with perfect placement of cleats. Ideal for hard fields.

**WEDGER***

Magnus Patented WEDGER* gives players a "balanced" toe and heel (see illustration) . . . thereby helping to eliminate Achilles tendon, arch and knee problems. WEDGER principle recommended as a valuable aid in treating a short heel cord. *U.S. PAT. 2904903

The "WEDGER" / OLD STYLE

Magnus/J.B. Athletic Shoe Company, *The Athletic Journal*, Mar.

42

**TENNIS SHOES**

Meet the individual needs of top professionals and amateurs with two styles, two action-proved soles, each perfected for a particular type of court. Full sponge insole, cushion heel and comfort arch.

**'Chuck' Taylor**
**ALL STARS**

World's No. 1 basketball shoe. Specified by more coaches, worn by more players than any other shoe expressly made for basketball. High cut or oxford. Used by the winning U.S. Olympic Team in Tokyo.

**TRACK STAR**

Indoors-outdoors favorite track shoe. Lightweight, trim-fitting, comfortable, a speed-inducing style that hugs the foot snugly in motion without chafing. Durable Army duck uppers; crepe rubber soles and heels.

**Correct decision,**
**for the fastest, surest feet in sports** ★

**WRESTLING SHOE**

A lightweight, exceptionally flexible shoe for quick footwork. Made extra high with white or black Army duck uppers for maximum protection. Concealed eyelets will not scratch mat. Non-marking molded outsole.

# converse ★ STAR QUALITY
ATHLETIC FOOTWEAR

## converse
### ... FOR THE WINNING MARGIN OF DIFFERENCE

**CONVERSE**
**TRACK STAR**

This light, comfortable, confident footing can make the winning fraction of difference. Designed to fit snugly without chafing, with durable army duck uppers and crepe rubber soles, the modestly priced TRACK STAR has become a year 'round favorite, indoors or out.

Sizes 1 to 14

**JACK KRAMER recommends**
**CONVERSE**
**TENNIS SHOES**

Split-second action and perfect traction are basic to a winning game. Jack Kramer wears and endorses the NO SLIP sole for dependable skidproof traction on grass, polished or damp courts. Choose it on the Lace-to-toe NET STAR or the Circular Vamp SKIDGRIP.

Men's sizes 4 to 14
Women's sizes 4 to 10

44

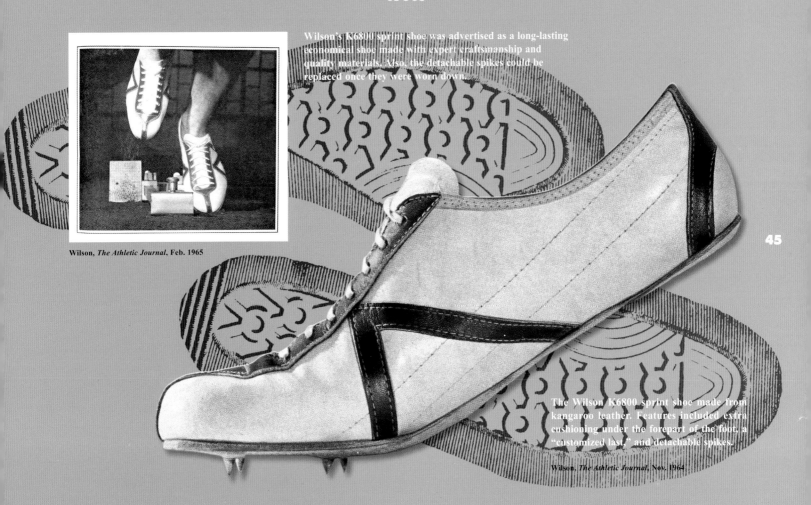

Wilson's K6800 sprint shoe was advertised as a long-lasting economical shoe made with expert craftsmanship and quality materials. Also, the detachable spikes could be replaced once they were worn down.

Wilson, *The Athletic Journal*, Feb. 1965

The Wilson K6800 sprint shoe made from kangaroo leather. Features included extra cushioning under the forepart of the foot, a "customized last," and detachable spikes.

Wilson, *The Athletic Journal*, Nov. 1964

45

The Wilson F9014 low-cut football shoe in blue-black kangaroo leather. Also available in a high-cut model.

Wilson, *The Athletic Journal*, Mar. 1965

46

Spalding's Featherweight Deluxe Sprint Shoe. Leather reinforcement bands and tapes along the sides and inside the shoe were included to prevent stretching. Sole leather was tanned twice for flexibility and durability.

Spalding, *The Athletic Journal*, Dec. 1964

Spalding, *The Athletic Journal*, Mar. 1965

Spalding's "Speed Model" Oxfords were designed with molded multi-studded outsoles, which were vulcanized and lock-stitched into place. Nylon-reinforced pull-up tabs at the arches allowed the shoes to be form-laced.

Spalding, *The Athletic Journal*, Mar. 1965

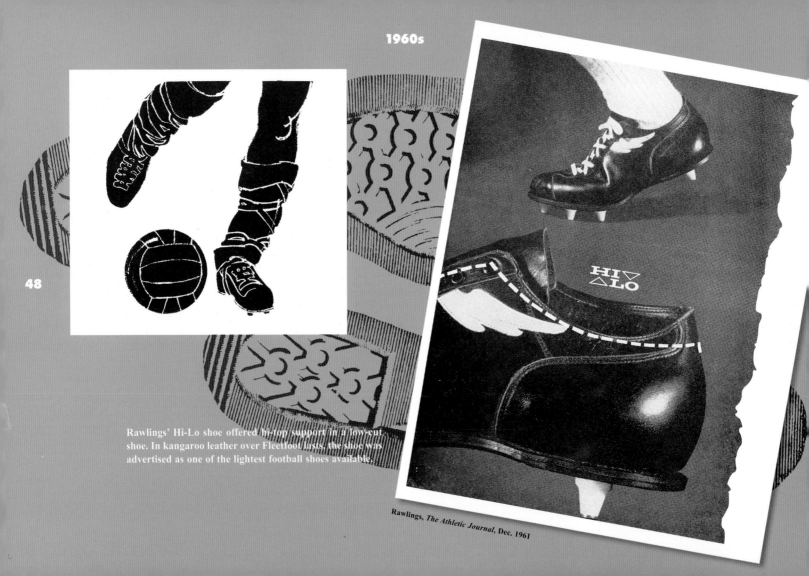

Rawlings' Hi-Lo shoe offered hi-top support in a low-cut shoe. In kangaroo leather over Fleetfoot lasts, the shoe was advertised as one of the lightest football shoes available.

Rawlings, *The Athletic Journal*, Dec. 1961

**Hyde Athletic Shoe Co.,** *The Athletic Journal*, Mar. 1962

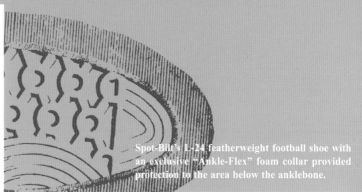

Spot-Bilt's L-24 featherweight football shoe with an exclusive "Ankle-Flex" foam collar provided protection to the area below the anklebone.

**Spot-Bilt,** *The Athletic Journal*, May 1965

The Hyde Lightweight 485 soccer boot in kangaroo leather with a shock absorbing rubber sole was moisture resistant. A roll-up rubber toe was supposed to improve footwork precision and a padded leather collar was included to protect the ankle and Achilles tendon.

High cut oxford cleats from Brooks with a grip lacing system. Nylon tapes extend from the arch to give extra support.

Brooks, *The Athletic Journal*, Sept. 1964

50

pressure free fit

**TWO ADIDAS TOP LINERS**
**adidas Model "2000"**
with the new relief sole and ac
heel-padding for a firm, comfortal
pressure-free fit. The heel protector as well as the adidas relief-sol
and studs are patented.
**adidas Telstar**
Top class model, 32 panels.
Flood-light ball white/black. Hand
sewn with nylon thread. Special
plastic coating.

form-fitting nylon-sole

adidas, *Soccer*, Summer 1969

Advertisements claimed adidas was the most popular soccer shoe in the world.

*adidas, Soccer, Spring 1969*

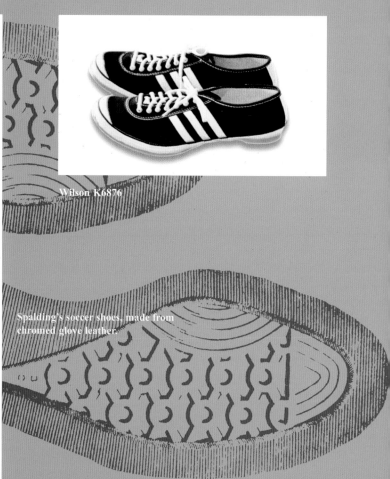

Wilson K6876

Spalding's soccer shoes, made from chromed glove leather.

Spalding, *Soccer*, Spring 1969

Wilson K6872

Wilson K6874

Wilson, *The Athletic Journal*, Jan. 1968

**Wilson K6882**

Wilson, *The Athletic Journal*, Jan. 1968

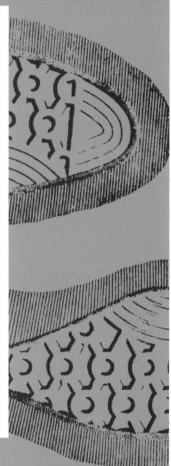

Saucony, *The Athletic Journal*, Nov. 1961

NE

less than 7 o

no lighter track meet shoe is mad
uppers of finest kangar

for NOVEMBER, 1961

Spot-Bilt's water resistant Speedster in white nylon mesh.

Spot-Bilt, *The Athletic Journal*, Oct. 1967

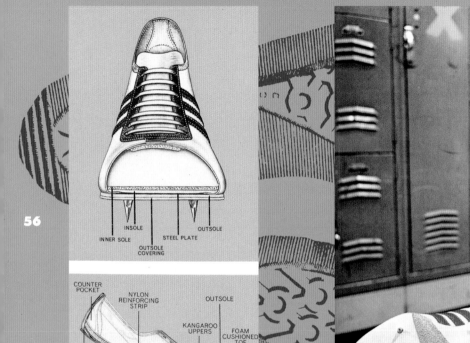

INNER SOLE    INSOLE    STEEL PLATE    OUTSOLE    OUTSOLE COVERING

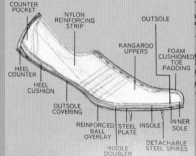

COUNTER POCKET    NYLON REINFORCING STRIP    OUTSOLE    KANGAROO UPPERS    FOAM CUSHIONED TOE PADDING    HEEL COUNTER    HEEL CUSHION    OUTSOLE COVERING    REINFORCED BALL OVERLAY    STEEL PLATE    INSOLE    INNER SOLE    INSOLE DOUBLER    DETACHABLE STEEL SPIKES

WILSON'S TROPHY WINNERS

*Wilson, The Athletic Journal, Oct. 1967*

Track shoes from Wilson.

Wilson, *The Athletic Journal*, Jan. 1968

# 1970s

Etonic/Charles Eaton Co., *Runner's World Magazine*

Dr. Rob Roy McGregor, Director of Runner's Clinic and Chief of Podiatry at the New England Deaconness hospital, worked as a consultant to help design the McGregor one-piece heal/arch support, the Charles Eaton Company's first running shoe.

58

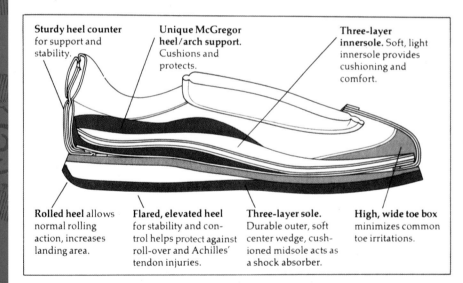

**Sturdy heel counter** for support and stability.

**Unique McGregor heel/arch support.** Cushions and protects.

**Three-layer innersole.** Soft, light innersole provides cushioning and comfort.

**Rolled heel** allows normal rolling action, increases landing area.

**Flared, elevated heel** for stability and control helps protect against roll-over and Achilles' tendon injuries.

**Three-layer sole.** Durable outer, soft center wedge, cushioned midsole acts as a shock absorber.

**High, wide toe box** minimizes common toe irritations.

Etonic/Charles Eaton Co., *Runner's World Magazine*

Etonic/Charles Eaton Co.,
*Runner's World Magazine*

Etonic/Charles Eaton Co., *Track & Field News*, Mar. 1978

**60**

# The 4¾ oz. racing shoe — by Patrick

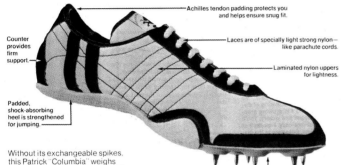

Achilles tendon padding protects you and helps ensure snug fit.

Counter provides firm support.

Laces are of specially light strong nylon— like parachute cords.

Laminated nylon uppers for lightness.

Padded, shock-absorbing heel is strengthened for jumping.

Strong light nylon sole has 6 replaceable steel spikes.

Without its exchangeable spikes, this Patrick "Columbia" weighs under 5 ounces. It's constructed in the way that nature constructs birds— for lightness throughout, and strength.

Which is why runners seem to fly in them. Athletes say, "We get good support all over the shoe." "When you lace it up the shoe really wraps up your foot." "It adapts."

Patrick athletic shoes are made in France, and have been known in Europe for over 25 years—for speed, styling, reliability. Other track shoes available in natural leather & suede. Run with Patrick and see how you take off.

**AL ACTION & LEISURE INC.**

45 East 30th St., N.Y. N.Y. 10016
Tel. (212) 686-8052

Patrick/Action & Leisure, Inc., *Runner's World Magazine*, May, 1975

# KINGSWELL TRACK 76/77

**516 Meteor**
Blue Split Leather
White trim, 4 spikes
**Sugg. Ret: $19.25**

**535 Arrow**
Suede Calf/Pigskin uppers, six
color combinations, 4 spikes
**Sugg. Ret: $22.30**

**527 Rapier**
Nylon uppers, Blue/White or
Red/White, 4 spikes
**Sugg. Ret: $24.50**

**547 Lance**
Nylon Uppers, Wedge Heel,
Blue/ Red, 4 spikes
**Sugg. Ret: $27.15**

Kingswell Sports U.S.A., *Runner's World Magazine*, Oct. 1976

**1130 ROAD RUNNER** — This design will absorb the continual stress of covering long distances on the road. BEIGE/RED. AVAILABLE IN SIZES 5½–13. $31.95 postpaid

**1977 MARATHON** — An extremely light training and racing shoe. BEIGE/RED. AVAILABLE IN SIZES 5½–13. $31.95 postpaid

**1144 SPURT** — Training shoe, with hard wearing herring bone pattern sole. BLUE/RED/GREEN. AVAILABLE IN SIZES 5½–13. $24.95 postpaid

**1810 JUNIOR** — Nylon training and racing shoe with cupped outer heel for stability. BLUE/RED/WHITE. AVAILABLE IN SIZES 5½–13. $18.95 postpaid

**1140 CHAMPION** — Nylon all purpose training shoe. WHITE/BLUE. AVAILABLE IN SIZES 5½–13. $29.95 postpaid

**1533 SPRINT** — Suction cup provides great traction on wet or dry surfaces. Interchangeable spike system. BLUE/RED/GREEN. AVAILABLE IN SIZES 5½–13. $27.95 postpaid

**1575 INTERVALL** — Pressure proof suction cup sole w/6 removable spikes. WHITE/GREEN. AVAILABLE IN SIZES 5½–13. $35.95 postpad

**1572 MUNICH** — Super light shoe. The new interchangeable six spike position together with newly developed suction cup sole. Provides great traction on wet or dry surfaces even under the most adverse conditions. RED. AVAILABLE IN SIZES 5½–13. $41.95 postpaid

**61**

# Reebok

**MADE IN ENGLAND**

**REINTRODUCING THE FAMOUS**

## WORLD TEN

Probably the World's most exclusive Marathon shoe. (Average shoe weight 5 oz.)
• Boston winner in record time.
• Olympic, European and Commonwealth Gold, Silver and Bronze medal winner.
• The green kid upper is fully lined and strengthened with anti-roll side patches. The World Ten has a cushion mid-sole, and long wear outer cover with cushion heel wedge and is beautifully balanced with glove-like fitting.

**$32·25**
Plus $1·00 Handling

### MARATHON
Super soft white cow hide trimmed in blue/orange with anti-roll side patches, deep cushion mid-sole, heel wedge and high traction long wearing outersole. A go anywhere shoe that gives a smooth, eventread.

**$26·75**
Plus $1·00 Handling

### COUGAR
Blue nylon, ½ lined with suede support at toe and around the heel. A superb nylon trainer, flat, with the same sole as the Marathon. Both shoes are fitted with arch supports and long wear innersocks.

**$25·60**
Plus $1·00 Handling

**STEP INTO BRITAINS LEADING ATHLETIC SHOE**
**SEND FOR YOURS TODAY**

**BRADFORD DISTRIBUTORS CORP. P.O. BOX 356 HUNTINGDON VALLEY P.A. 19006**

**AREA DISTRIBUTORS** We Require Distributors In The South, Midwest, Northwest, and Southwest States. For Full Details Write To Reebok International Ltd. Bolton Rd. Bury, Lancs. England.

**The 1919 Sao Paulo from Lydiard. Available in blue with white.**

**Lydiard,** *Runner's World Magazine,* Aug. 1975

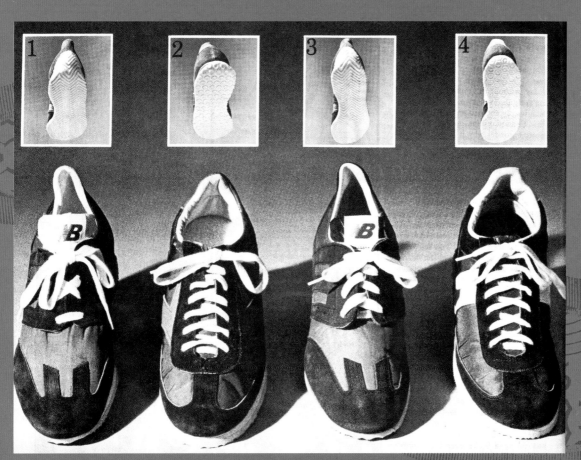

From left: New Balance 320 in blue nylon with high heel pad and a nylon tongue; Brooks Villanova II; New Balance 305, lighter than the 320 with a thinner sole; and Etonic's first running shoe.

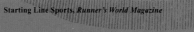

Starting Line Sports, *Runner's World Magazine*

Osaga, *Runner's World Magazine*, October

COSMO
Available January
Suggested Retail
Price: $26.00
in nylon

MOSCOW 80
Available January
Suggested Retail
Price: $27.00 Boys
$28.00 Mens

WOMEN'S TRAINER
Available January
Suggested Retail
Price: $28.00

COUGAR
Top Children's traini
Available now
Suggested Re
$8.00 In
$9.00 Yo

you pay for the sho
not the "big nam
who wears i

Many shoe companies spend large sums of money to e
that their shoes are worn in the big races.
We put our money into the shoe itself for the benefit of
biggest race of all. You.

OSAGA. for the
human race.

64

This tennis shoe was advertised as everything
Arthur Ashe ever wanted for his feet. The sneakers
featured raised heels, holes for ventilation, nylon
stitching, and extra reinforcement in the toes to
prevent tearing.

Head Tennis Division, *Tennis*, July 1971

SPRINT SPIKE

SPEED FLAT

DISTANCE SPIKE

TARTAN SPIKE

LONG JUMP

HAMMER THROW

JAVELIN BOOT

DISCUS

HIGH JUMP

RALLY TRAINING FLAT

SHOT PUT

TRIPLE JUMP

Diadora sneakers were made with natural gum rubber soles and uppers of nylon, baby veal, leather, or wild boar.

Diadora, *Track & Field News*, July 1978

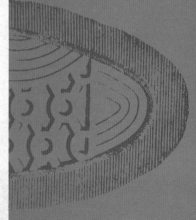

HIGHLY RANKED # MULTIPLIER
MADE IN TAIWAN

P.O. BOX 36-167 TAIPEI
TELEX: 21453 TAIPEI
TEL: (02)7516922, (02)7410357

MENTION ENTERPRISES & CO., LTD.

Mention Enterprises & Co., Ltd., *Track & Field News*, Jan. 1976

**Medallist training flats.**

**Medallist Athletic Shoes,** *Runner's World Magazine*

**KARHU**—The finest manufacturers of athletic shoes. Latest improved styles, quality-made, soft flexible nylon and leather uppers. The best in the industry—made in FINLAND.

**No. 2323.** The finest nylon, leather-trimmed marathon, training, cross-country shoes on the market today. Lightweight, comfortable, 3/4" heel, rubber arch and insole, padded achilles. This is the best. Sizes 5-13.

Our price: $25.95

**No. 2310.** Most comfortable and extra sturdy leather uppers. Great for all purposes—marathons, training, etc. Best I have seen. Sizes 5 to 13.

Our price: $19.75

**No. 24.** These are the best leisure shoes on the market. Finest suede leathers, padded in all the important places. Colors available: blue, gold, tan, red, brown. Sizes 3 to 13.

Our price: $17.95

**No. HJ-200.** Nylon uppers, leather trim. Triple sole. Corrugated new style, long-wearing. Full suede leather over toe, sides and back. We are direct importers; savings are substantial. Red, blue, gold. Sizes 4 to 13.

Sale price: $10.95

**No. 161. Puma "Crack" (Flipper).** 585 pairs Puma "Crack" in royal blue only. Sizes 10, 10½, 11, 11½, 12, 12½, 13 only. Retail price: $24.95

Our sale price: $15.75

**No. S.J.G. MacGregor.** First quality shoes. Full grain white leather uppers with 4 stripes. Your choice of blue or green stripes. Padded at ankle and heel. Padded arch support. Molded long-wearing rubber soles. Excellent for training, jogging, gym. Sizes 7 to 12.

School price: $15.95
Our sale: $9.75

**No. 146.** Made in France by Patrick. A fine leisure shoe. Strong, non-slip suction sole. Royal, gold, brown, navy, blue jean, scarlet. Sizes 5 to 13. Retail price: $25.00.

Sale price: $15.95

**No. 511.** Made in France by Patrick. New, improved, lightweight training shoe. Double corrugated sole. Nylon and leather covered uppers. Royal blue or scarlet. Sizes 7 to 13.

Sale price: $16.85

Carlsen Import Shoe Corp., *Runner's World Magazine*, Oct. 1975

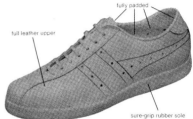
Gola/General Sportcraft Co. Ltd., *Tennis*, May 1975

**67**

68

# You've got all summer to find a better basketball shoe.

Oxford style 08
High shoe style 09

## BATA BULLETS will save you the time.

## America's fastest long distance movers.

Bata Bullets Cross Country Racers.

Long-wearing, durable track shoes that help you go the distance in winning time. Mens and boys sizes and colors of red, white or black with multi-color stripes.

Best of all, they're priced economically. You can put your entire squad into Amer-

ica's fastest, long distance movers and easily pay the freight. Also available in deluxe Pro Model featuring terry-cloth lining, double foxing and drill bindings.

Be ready for the long run. Contact your local sporting goods dealer. For the fastest move to the finish line.

**Bata BULLETS**
MADE IN USA

Division of Bata Shoe Company, Inc., Belcamp, Maryland

**Bata Shoe Co., Inc.,** *The Athletic Journal,* Nov. 1970

**Bata Bullets,** basketball shoes with canvas uppers and moulded Footbed® insoles for perfect support and balance. The insoles were treated to prevent rotting, infection, and odor.

**Bata Shoe Co.,** *The Athletic Journal,* June 1971

adidas, *Runner's World Magazine*

These adidas track shoes featured interchangeable
elements for optimal performance.

From left: Laplata, Speed, Superlight. Below: University, Star
Streak, and Turf Streak by adidas.

adidas, *The Athletic Journal*, Dec. 1970

PUT YOUR FOOT INTO ADIDAS!

An important way that adidas takes care of the fitness and health of all athletes: SL 76 – a new fabulous training shoe developed in consultation with sports physicians. Because of the outstanding orthopaedic features they are a must for all long distance runners and for physical training. Truly, all the latest technical advantages are built into the model SL 76.

adidas, *Track & Field News*, June 1975

The adidas Marathon racing shoe featured a special goatskin upper and revolutionary midsole with extra shock-absorption. The shoe also featured a heel counter and padded Achilles tendon protector.

Adidas, *Runner's World Magazine*, Aug. 1974

The adidas SL 72 and Country were developed in conjunction with sports physicians to include orthopedic features for long distance runners and general physical training.

# TREAT YOUR FEET!

For sprinters or long distance runners adidas treats your feet with a standard of excellence that is often imitated, but never duplicated.

"SL '72" and "Country" Both adidas-models have been developed in consultation with sports physicians. Because of the outstanding orthopedic features they are a must for all long distance runners and for general physical training. Another way that adidas takes care of the fitness and health of all athletes.

adidas, *Track & Field News*, Feb. 1974

adidas, *Runner's World Magazine*, Aug. 1975

**The adidas Runner, a special training shoe for long-distance runners.**

Pressure-free foot-form tongue

Cushioning around in step area

Practical easy lace system

Special padding for protection of heel and Achilles tendon

Uppers easy-to-breath wide mesh nylon

Thick hell wedge for a truly cushioned run

Built-in fulcrum at the ball of foot to assist in easy rolling action

Orthopedic arch suppord is built in

Durable star profile sole

adidas, *Runner's World Magazine*

The Superstar and Promodel, white leather basketball shoes from adidas.

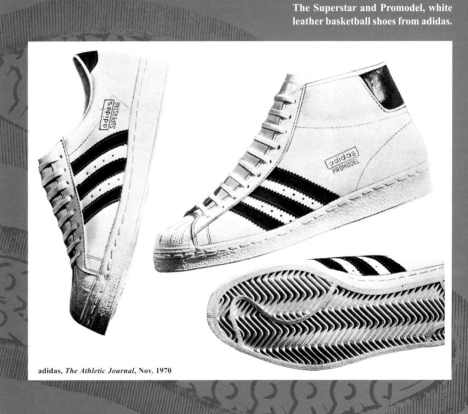

adidas, *The Athletic Journal*, Nov. 1970

WIMBLEDON. Very flexible.
Superlight. Very flexible.
Soft white kangaroo uppers
with blue-red-blue stripes.
SOFTPROTECT. Herring bone sole,
perforated tongue and uppers.

JOHN NEWCOMBE
The very moderate
price makes
this model acceptable
for all.
Oxhide uppers.
Heel counter provides
a secure fit.
Very durable shell sole.

ROD LAVER
Designed in collaboration
with Rod Laver.
The only tennis shoe
with ventilated nylon uppers.
SOFTPROTECT. New improved
vulcanized gum rubber sole.

• SOFTPROTECT:
perfect protection of ankle heel
and achilles tendon.

adidas Rod Laver
Light,
comfortable,
solid,
washable,
ventilated,
absorbent.

adidas Lady
New attractive
top class-model.

adidas Haillet
Soft and safe,
more solid,
more comfortable,
than any
other shoe.

adidas, *Tennis*, Nov. 1971

adidas, *Tennis*, July 1970

adidas, *Tennis*, Aug. 1971

# Game, Set and Match for adidas

adidas –
on top of the tennis world.
*First choice*
with the leading players.
Rod Laver –
John Newcombe –
Stan Smith –
Marty Riessen –
Billie King –
Rosemary Casals –
and the list goes on.

"Davis Cup"
A super-light and
very flexible tennis shoe.
A top class leather upper
with adidas dish-sole.

DAVIS-CUP

"Rod Laver"
The only tennis shoe
with ventilated
nylon uppers.
Vulcanized
gum-rubber sole.

**adidas**

The Rod Laver adidas tennis shoes with nylon uppers were designed to absorb perspiration. Rod Laver was an Australian tennis champion.

The preformed sole of an adidas Haillet tennis shoe with padded heal.

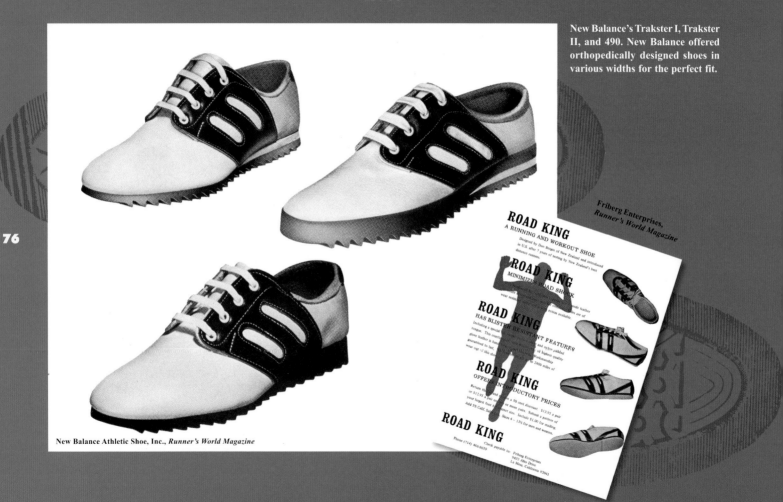

New Balance's Trakster I, Trakster II, and 490. New Balance offered orthopedically designed shoes in various widths for the perfect fit.

*Friberg Enterprises,
Runner's World Magazine*

New Balance Athletic Shoe, Inc., *Runner's World Magazine*

**ROAD KING**
A RUNNING AND WORKOUT SHOE

**ROAD KING**
MINIMIZES ROAD SHOCK

**ROAD KING**
HAS BLISTER RESISTANT FEATURES

**ROAD KING**
OFFERS INTRODUCTORY PRICES

**ROAD KING**

76

New Balance Speedsters in
bright blue with a red saddle.

New Balance Athletic Shoe, Inc., *Runner's World Magazine*

New Balance Athletic Shoe, Inc., *Runner's World Magazine*

The speedster running flat from New Balance,
made from a lightweight nylon upper with suede
leather toe piece. Advertised as offering more toe
room in addition to a full length midsole, heel
wedge, and shock-neutralizing innersole.

New Balance Athletic Shoe, Inc., Runner's World Magazine, Apr. 1976

# New Balance Special Sale

For a limited time, we're offering three sports shoes at very special prices. Each of these has the unique New Balance width sizing (3½ to 15, AA to EEE) and is an orthopedically designed shoe suited to both men and women. Get twice the shoe now for about half the price.

**360A** An all-purpose sports shoe, the 360A has a lightweight, comfortable, soft suede upper and a Cushion-crepe sole designed to be light yet durable. Perfect for light jogging, tennis, or casual wear, in royal blue with white trim. Formerly $22.95; now just $13.

**Head Courtster** Ideal for all playing surfaces, the lightweight Head Courtster features an all white leather upper and a reinforced toe, with full foxing and a smooth but durable Cushion-crepe sole. Formerly $24.95; now just $12. Widths EE and EEE not available.

**Courtster** Designed for the aggressive tennis player on all court surfaces, the Courtster offers padded binding, a heel counter, and a tough gum-tread outer sole in addition to its white leather upper, full foxing, and reinforced toe. Formerly $24.95; now just $12. Widths EE and EEE not available.
- - - - - - - - - - - - - -

New Balance offered sneakers in different widths for the perfect fit. Unlike other sneakers, New Balances laced only to the saddle over the instep to keep from restricting toes.

**Interval 3:05** The ultimate training shoe, weighing only 9½ oz. yet durable enough for road racing. Leather-reinforced nylon upper with flocked nylon lining. Protective midsole plus heel-elevating softee wedge to reduce extension of the Achilles tendon and cushion the leg. Flared heel to stabilize the foot during heel strike and reduce ankle-roll injuries. Men and women, 3½ AA to 15 EEE, in Navy blue with white trim.

**2:05** Ideal for training and speed work, and now made of tough, lightweight pigskin with shock-absorbing, molded Kraton® sole. Reverse ripples for added traction and shock absorption. Rolled heel to stabilize the foot during heel strike. Men and women, 3½ AA to 15 EEE, in Kelly green with tan trim or Royal blue with white trim.

**Trackster III** The most protective of all training shoes, with a molded Ripple® sole to absorb up to 40 percent of road shock. Unique foxing construction for greater lateral stability, and foot-conforming soft suede upper for comfort. Men and women, 3½ AA to 15 EEE, in Royal blue with white trim.

**Competition** The totally new idea in racing shoes: a perfect fit for maximum performance. Width sizing, plus ultra-light 7½ oz. weight. Knobby sole for excellent traction on all surfaces, and New Balance's unique-at-the-price wedge/midsole combination to keep weight forward and absorb shock. Men and women, 3½ AA to 15 EEE, in Royal blue with white trim. The shoe that placed third in the Boston Marathon.

New Balance Athletic Shoe, Inc., Runner's World Magazine, July 1975

Puma, *Tennis*, June 1974

These Pumas' anatomically molded soles were designed for a better fit. The shoes' design also featured foam padding at the heel, ankle, and sponge sole, together with arch support and deep-set sole tread designs.

Special long wearing treads on the tough rubber soles, thick foam wedge tapering, ankle and Achilles tendon pads, and leather reinforced nylon uppers were some of the features of the Puma Super Long Distance Shoes. Available in red, blue, and yellow.

Puma, *Runner's World Magazine*, Oct. 1975

Tiger sneakers with durable nylon uppers, a wider heel, and a leather toe cap offered miles of safe running.

Tiger, *Runner's World Magazine*, July1975

80

The Tiger Jayhawk (left) had gum rubber "suction tread" for extra traction. Good for training or casual wear in bright yellow with navy stripes. The Tiger Ohbori, advertised as an excellent marathon shoe, was built on a spike last in navy with yellow stripes.

Tiger, *Runner's World Magazine*, Sept. 1975

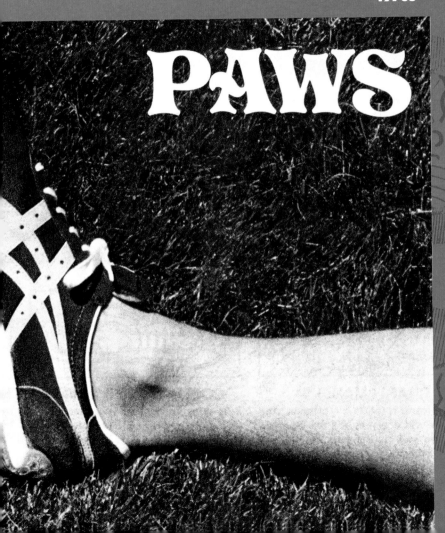

**From top:** Tiger's TG-4 Marathon with all nylon uppers; TG-22 Road Runner with lightweight buffed calf uppers; and Olympiade XIX with all nylon uppers.

Tiger, *Track & Field News*, Aug. 1975

**The G-33 Spartan B and T-30 Leather Semi Ripple from Tiger.**

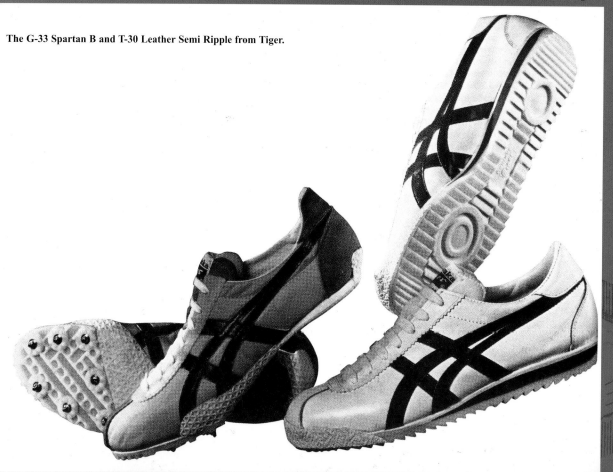

new from
Spot-bilt
**the All-American**

Spot-Bilt's All-American BK-70 leather basketball shoe was "designed for the wider American foot," featuring a stitched and cemented outsole.

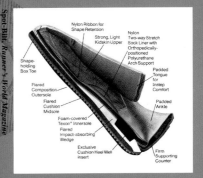

Nylon Ribbon for Shape Retention

Strong, Light Kidskin Upper

Nylon Two-way Stretch Sock Liner with Orthopedically-positioned Polyurethane Arch Support

Shape-holding Box Toe

Padded Tongue for Instep Comfort

Flared Composition Outersole

Flared Cushion Midsole

Foam-covered Texon° Innersole

Flared Impact-absorbing Wedge

Exclusive Cushion Heel Well insert

Padded Ankle

Firm Supporting Counter

Spot-Bilt's Style 880 was advertised as containing a special heel design to protect the heel and ankle.

**83**

## The **Dove** 8860N

### THE IDEAL TRAINING FLAT
### FOR THE SERIOUS WOMAN RUNNER

### Rated by **Runner's World**
as the *top shoe in its category*

**All the performance features of SAUCONY'S finest men's training flats combined in a moderately priced shoe for women athletes.**

- Built-up heel
- Soft, lightweight nylon upper
- Long-lasting, two layer suction cup sole
- Achilles tendon protector
- Rolled heel and toe
- Padded tongue and heel support
- Built-in arch support
- Full heel counter for firm fit
- Flexible
- Lightweight

Saucony, *Runner's World Magazine*

**5530N Ms. Coach**

The perfect all-around shoe for both coach and cheerleader.

**8823N Venus**

Lightweight women's track spike.

**8870 Spikette**

For the no-nonsense female volleyball player.

**0140 Ms. Star**

A quality all-purpose shoe for the woman athlete — for field hockey, soccer, softball, etc.

Saucony, *Runner's World Magazine*

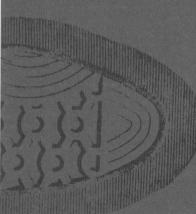

Nike/The Athletic Department; Runner's *World Magazine*, Aug. 1975

Nike, *Track & Field News,* Jan. 1975

# NIKE

## OREGON WAFFLE

Nike's Oregon Waffle was developed by Bill Bowerman, 1972 Olympic coach, to have the traction of a spiked shoe, but the comfort of a flat one. The legendary first waffle sole was said to be made in Bill Bowerman's waffle iron, glued onto the bottom of running shoe, and tested by athletes.

From top: Nike's Waffle Trainer with a flared sole and undercut heel provided stability and improved footstrike; Oregon Waffle in bright yellow with green trim; and an older version of the Waffle Trainer in blue nylon.

From top: Nike's Flyte Wet in top grade leather coated with a shiny layer of polyurethane for a unique look; Nylon Cortez 1; and Super Cortez in leather.

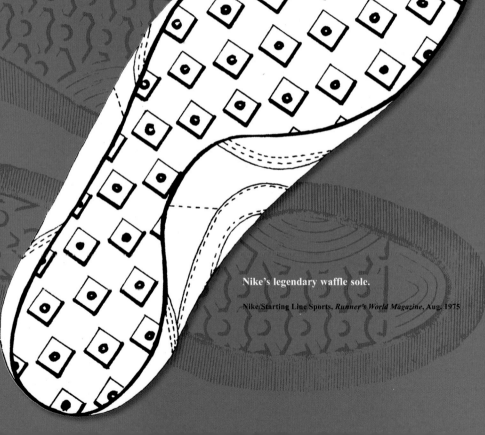

Nike's legendary waffle sole.

Nike/Starting Line Sports, *Runner's World Magazine*, Aug. 1975

## 1. Waffle Trainer

This revolutionary trainer combines all the padding of a training shoe with the lightness of a racing flat. The flared sole and undercut heel provide stability and help insure proper footstrike and toe-off. 27.95 team 22.95

## 3. Americas

Nike's most popular competition spike. Nylon uppers make them light enough to race in and tough enough to train in. The hundreds of tiny cones on the sole provide sure traction on all surfaces. 29.95 team 24.50

## 5. Cortez

The Nike "standard" training and jogging shoes. (5a) "Leather Deluxe" is the top of the line, sizes 3-13, 27.95 team 22.95; (5b) Suede Deluxe, 3-13, 27.95 team 22.95; (5c) Nylon. Foul weather special, 3-13, 24.95 team 20.75; (5d) Leather, 3-13, great for young runners. 23.95 team 19.95; (5e) Senorita, women's sizes 4-10 24.95 team 20.25.

## 2. Oregon Waffle

The Shoe made famous in Eugene, Oregon. This racing shoe has a bright yellow nylon upper with green trim. The unique Waffle sole provides traction on any surface. It combines the traction of a spike with the cushion of a flat. This may be the most sophisticated racing flat ever made. 24.95 team 19.95

## 4. Intervalles

Weather resistant nylon uppers with a raised heel wedge provide protection against heel bruises and Achilles strain. This training shoe has turned out to be a favorite racing shoe for many runners. 26.95 team 22.25

## 6. Finland Blue or Kenya Red

One of the most popular training shoes available anywhere. Nylon uppers and herringbone sole make this training shoe surprisingly light. Padded ankle collar and cushioned foam midsole insure miles of comfort. 22.95 team 18.95

Nike/The Athletic Department, *Runner's World Magazine*, Oct. 1975

Nike made the Cortez in three different styles of uppers: buffed leather, nylon, or suede. Notice the "anti-wear plug" at the heel, which was intended for extra wear. The Cortez was available with an extra wide toe for runners with problem feet. The shoe was originally designed in the mid-1960s by Olympic coach Bill Bowerman for long distance runners.

88

Nike/The Athletic Department, *Runner's World Magazine*

NEW Features for the 70's:

"Anti-wear plug" at heel for miles of extra wear.

Choice of 3 styles of uppers for optimal comfort and styling; buffed leather, nylon or suede.

4-way stretch inner-soles for added comfort and blister protection.

Extra-wide toe available for the runner with problem feet.

Nike's Kenya Reds with weather-resistant
"swooshfiber" uppers, midsole cushions, heel wedges,
and high density herringbone outer soles.

Nike/The Athletic Department, *Runner's World Magazine*

The "boston '73" by Nike was originally the Obori, but
was renamed in commemoration of the 1973 Boston
Marathon, when four of the top seven winners wore
these sneakers. The boston '73 was advertised as hav-
ing "the most complete ball-to-heel instep support found
in any running shoe."

Nike/Blue Ribbon Sports, *Runner's World Magazine*, Aug. 1973

Converse All Stars® tennis shoes in suede glove leather uppers with padded tongue and ankle collar.

Converse's four classic tennis shoe models with canvas tops: the Skidgrip, Net Star, Net King, and Court star, and two All Stars® in suede or leather.

90

Converse, *Tennis*, Apr. 1972

Converse, *Tennis*, Jan. 1971

Converse, *Tennis*, Feb. 1972

Converse All Stars® tennis shoe.

New Zealand native Arthur B. Lydiard developed the design for the E.B. Sport International "Arthur Lydiard Road Runner." Features included a multi-layered sole and heel cushioning, cupped heel and arch support, and weather-resistant gray suede leather uppers. Arthur Lydiard, a New Zealand native, was a renowned running coach and Olympic athlete.

Converse All Stars® tennis shoe.

Converse, *Tennis*, Feb. 1972

E.B. Sport International/*Runner's World, Runner's World Magazine*

**92**

Wide flared heel gives greater running stability and increased wear.

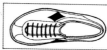

E.B. Sport International, *Runner's World Magazine*

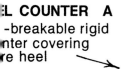

**UPPER SOFTNESS  A**
Blue Nylon upper with
leather reinforced toe
and heel

L COUNTER  A
-breakable rigid
nter covering
e heel

**VARIABLE WIDTHS  A**
Narrow   8-11
Medium   4-13
Wide     8-11

**SHOE WEIGHT  B**
11 ozs.—ideal training
shoe weight

L LIFT  A
nick soft crepe
dropping to ½"
all

HANK SUPPORT  A
olid shank

**INSIDE SUPPORT  A**
Built-in orthopedic
arch support covered
with sponge

**SOLE BEND  A**
Special flexibility at
ball normally found in
racing shoes

**SOLE MAKE-UP  A**
2 layer sole—½" thick
at ball

Brooks/The Athletic Attic, *Runner's World Magazine*

The Villanova II by Brooks with a flared heel for extra stability and durability.

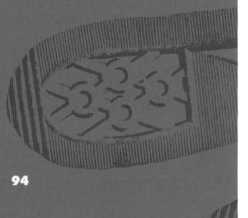

94

# 4 track & field

### american (Left)

Tough leather uppers help equip this shoe with all the necessities for long distance training. The soles propel the runner toward his goal by providing positive forward traction. This shoe is just like the people it's named after— rugged, dependable and able to bounce back after an exhausting challenge.

### sting (Top middle)

A marathon runner needs all the help he can get to withstand this particularly grueling race. STING is specially designed as a racing marathon shoe. It gives the athlete DENYAFOUR nylon uppers and a tough sole that supports his feet over any terrain during the long, brutal races.

### moscow '80 (Bottom middle)

This shoe is constructed of DENYA-FOUR fiber and is designed to reduce leg injuries with its nylon heel counter that's joined to a soft midsole and wedge. The M-'80 gives extra toe and metatorsal area and has a tough wearing sole. This footwear allows the athlete to attack his training in comfort.

### comfort plus (Right)

The comfort of the athlete was in mind when this shoe was designed. It has DENYAFOUR uppers and features a rounded toe for added room. Suede reinforcement gives needed support to problem areas and long wearing gum soles provide positive forward traction when it's most needed.

**point 4our ltd.**
4050 Talmadge Road
Toledo, Ohio 43623
(419) 472-6982

Point Four Ltd., *Runner's World Magazine*, Aug. 1975

Point Four, Ltd., *Runner's World Magazine*, July 1975

*Riddell, The Athletic Journal, Mar. 1971*

**Riddell's football cleats with nylon soles.**

*Wilson, Soccer, Winter 1970*

Brine, *The Athletic Journal*, June 1971

Brine's Cheetah soccer cleats.

*Stubert*

Stubert football shoe in black chrome cowhide with polyurethane soles.

Stubbs & Burt Ltd., *Soccer*, Spring 1971

Stylo Matchmakers International, Inc., *Soccer*, Fall 1975

**PADDED COLLAR**
Snug comfort at
heel and ankle

**PADDED TONGUE**
No "bind" across
the instep

**DISTINCTIVE
STYLING**
Plus superb British
craftsmanship

**MOLDED
MULTI-CLEAT SOLE**
or polyurethane sole
with replaceable cleats

**"PERM-ARCH"**
Extra support where
needed most

**GENUINE LEATHER**
Soft to wear, yet
amazingly tough

**Stylo Matchmakers were all-purpose athletic shoes.**

**The Puma Pele King soccer cleat with polyurethane sole, padded ankle and tendon pad, black leather upper, and a yellow stripe. Named after famed soccer player Pele, who helped to develop the shoe's design.**

Puma, *Soccer*, Spring 1971

THE CHALLENGING LINE

STYLE SSL
H6542

STYLE SSR
H6572

STYLE SSR
H6562

STYLE SSL
H6522

STYLE SSV
H6552

STYLE SSV
H6532

H6682

H6683

H6684

98

Soccer apparel and
shoes by Wilson.

Wilson, *Soccer*, Fall 1969 Insert

# OF SOCCER APPAREL

STYLE SPML

STYLE SPSL

H6370

H6582

F9060

H6580
STYLE SSV

F9062

C1362

H6912

F4835

H6922

Gola/Sportcraft Co., Ltd., *Soccer*, Summer 1976

100

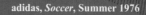

Gola soccer cleats advertised by Sportcraft.

adidas, *Soccer*, Summer 1976

THE HOME OF SOCCER

NO. 137

NO. 504

NO. 515

TEL-STAR

THE
FINEST
FROM
AROUND
THE
WORLD

NO. 707

WORLD CUP

Soccer Sport Supply Co., Inc., *Soccer*, Summer 1976

Viking football, training, and tennis shoes.

Soccer Sport Supply Co., Inc., *Soccer*, Spring 1970

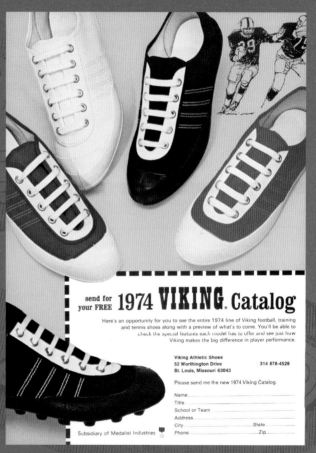

send for your FREE **1974 VIKING Catalog**

Here's an opportunity for you to see the entire 1974 line of Viking football, training and tennis shoes along with a preview of what's to come. You'll be able to check the special features each model has to offer and see just how Viking makes the big difference in player performance.

**Viking Athletic Shoes**
52 Worthington Drive
St. Louis, Missouri 63043        314 878-4528

Please send me the new 1974 Viking Catalog.

Name
Title
School or Team
Address
City _____ State
Phone _____ Zip

Subsidiary of Medalist Industries

Viking Athletic Shoes, *The Athletic Journal*, May 1974

These Converse shoes were made exclusively for Sears in a variety of solid colors and stripes.

Converse/Sears, *The Athletic Journal*, Sept. 1973

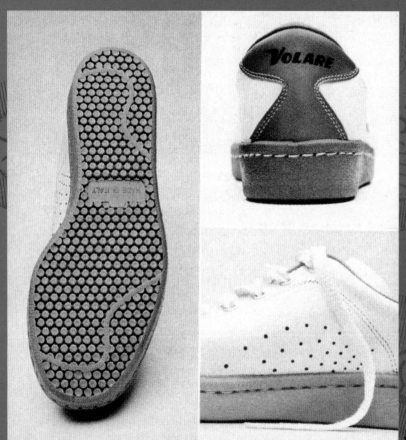

Volare, *Tennis*, Jan. 1975

Volare's tennis shoes were available in five bright colors: royal blue, forest green, sunshine yellow, ruby red, and classic white. Padded rims, raised tendon protectors, and firm arch supports are among the features listed for the leather shoes.

Volare, *Tennis*, Jan. 1975

Asahi, *Tennis*, May 1976

These Asahi tennis shoe uppers were made in "slow cure" ovens after the soles and shoe bodies were fastened together by hand. According to this ad, the slow manufacturing process led to a higher quality shoe. The multi-layered traction grid rubber soles were also listed as a feature that added to the shoes' durability.

Pony tennis shoes were built for "the American foot" with extra room at the toe.

Pony, *Tennis*, Oct. 1975

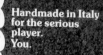
Lotto tennis shoes were handmade in Italy.

106

Lotto, *Tennis*, June 1976

Bancroft Tretorn tennis shoes, in canvas or leather, were imported from Sweden. They were advertised for on the court and off.

Bancroft Tretorn, *Tennis*, Mar. 1976

Penn Tennis/Athletic Products Division General Tire, *Tennis*, May 1974

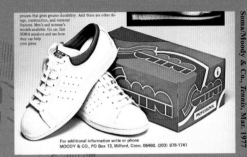

*Soma/Moody & Co., Tennis, Mar. 1977*

The Soma tennis shoe was developed after two years of research and testing. In full grain leather with special construction for extra durability.

Leather Penn Royal Court Shoes for men.

*Bata Shoe Co., Inc., Tennis, Dec. 1974*

**108**

Bata's Poly Love tennis shoe for women was made with polyurethane to keep it lightweight, and came in a variety of colors.

Bata Shoe Co., Inc., *Tennis*, June 1974

Jack Purcell/B.F. Goodrich, *Tennis,* Mar. 1972

The Tournament Purcell with weightless Dacron® uppers and non-skid herringbone soles, not to mention "exclusive Posture Foundation support for tireless, point-winning poise."

Jack Purcell/B.F. Goodrich, *Tennis,* June 1970

Jack Purcell's Coolaire, Closed Vamp, RaceAround, and Lace-to-Toe. An advertisement quoted Cliff Richey, tennis shoe pro, as saying that the insoles were the toughest around.

Blue Laurel wreaths adorned these Fred Perry tennis shoes by Eaton. Raised heels and an extra cushioned collar and tongue were added to a lightweight and durable one-piece construction in this "three-time Wimbledon winner."

Fred Perry/Eaton, *Tennis*, May 1967

Foot-Joy, Inc., *Tennis*, Jan. 1977

# Let a Pro show you how to play mixed doubles.

Foot-Joys met the quality standards of tennis pro shops. This ad named the company number one in golf shoes. Made with skill and craftsmanship since 1857.

According to this ad, Fred Perry tennis shoes were worth the extra cost, in canvas and leather.

Fred Perry/Eaton, *Tennis*, May 1975

The Tred 2-Z was marketed as a specialty racquetball or handball sports shoe. A gum rubber sole contributed to the shoe's light weight, and an extended leather toe was reinforced with extra stitching for extra durability. Perfect traction for wooden floors, mesh sides, and special negative heel with cup were other features touted by this ad.

Tred 2, *Tennis*, Sept. 1977

## Introducing the Tred 2 tennis shoe.

RECESSED INSTEP AREA TO REDUCE WEIGHT

Tred 2, Inc., 2504 Channing Avenue, San Jose, Ca 95131

Tred 2, *Tennis*, Mar. 1976

Tred 2, *Track & Field News*, June 1979

"The TRED 2 Double D.™ Because your foot wants the best of two shoes when it can only wear one, " said this ad. The Double D stands for "Double Durometer," a midsole innovation of Tred 2's that provided a firm sole and a soft sole at the same time – with firm cushioning at the heel, softer and more flexible cushioning towards the front for a more comfortable fit. The light nylon uppers were reinforced with suede.

Another view of the PRO-Keds Trophy Deluxe tennis shoe.

Pro-Keds, *Tennis*, May 1976

114

PRO-Keds Trophy Deluxe tennis shoes came in yellow, blue, green, or white.

# TO GET TO THE TOP, YOU'VE GOT TO START AT THE BOTTOM.

In tennis, you need all the help you can get.

So to give you a hand, Pro-Keds® came up with the thing. For your feet.

It's called the Trophy Deluxe. And with its padded tongue and collar, protective toe bumper and the choice of fabric or leather, you'll find all the things that have made us famous for winning.

And, come to think of it, all the things that might keep you from losing.

**UNIROYAL**

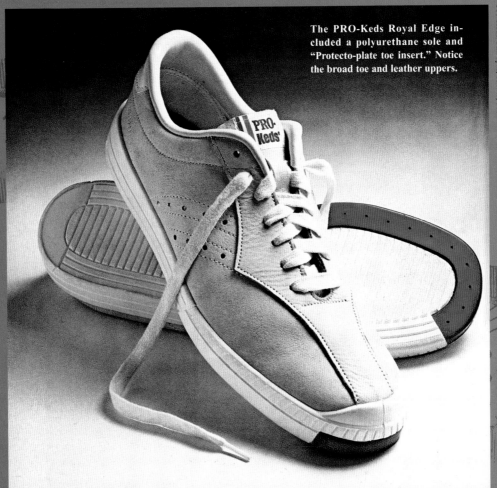

The PRO-Keds Royal Edge included a polyurethane sole and
"Protecto-plate toe insert." Notice
the broad toe and leather uppers.

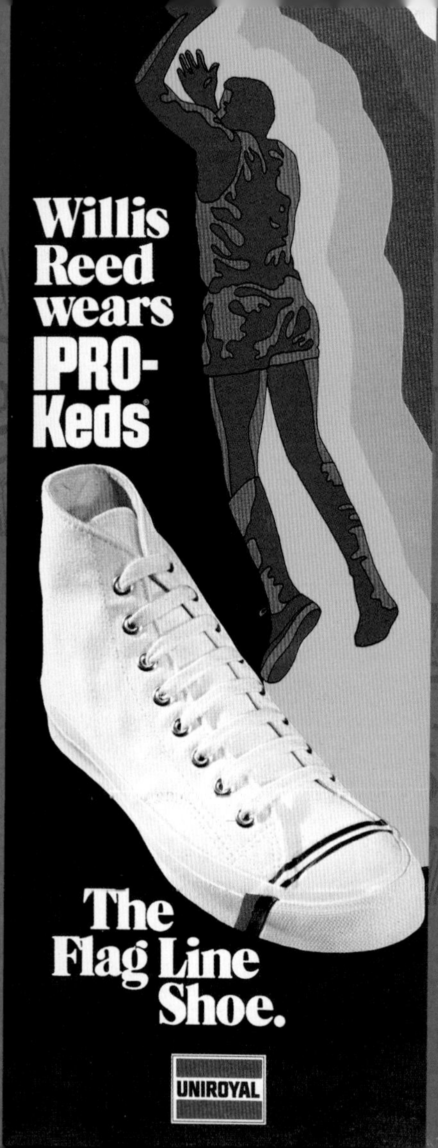

116

Willis
Reed
wears
**PRO-
Keds**®

The
Flag Line
Shoe.

UNIROYAL

Pro-Keds/Uniroyal, The Athletic Journal, Nov. 1973

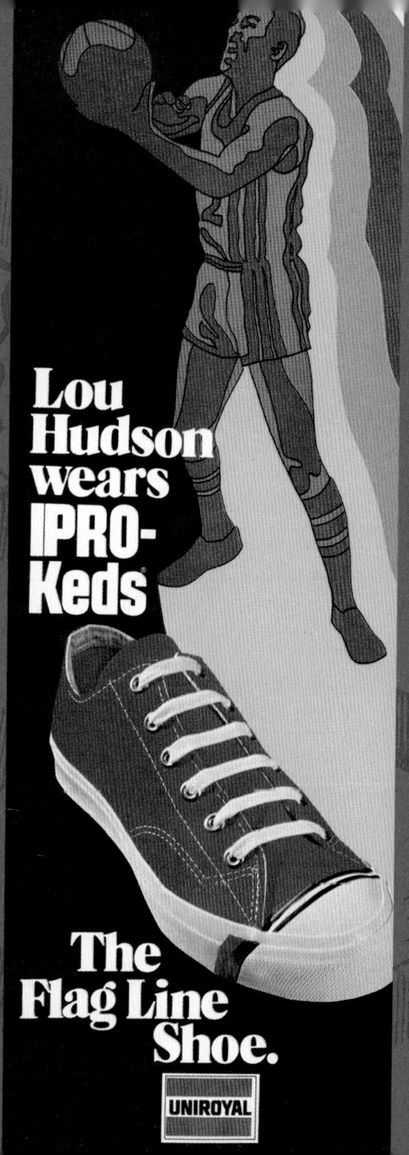

Lou
Hudson
wears
**PRO-
Keds**®

The
Flag Line
Shoe.

UNIROYAL

Pro-Keds, Uniroyal, The Athletic Journal, Sept. 1973

adidas, *Track & Field News*, Mar. 1979

adidas, *Track & Field News*, Mar. 1979

**117**

According to advertising, the Adidas TRX Competition could never have been designed without the help of runners. An incredibly light and stable shoe, with a studded sole for extra traction. "The science of sport" appears written below the ad's adidas logo.

# Look at the feet...

adidas, *The Athletic Journal*, Sept. 1973

adidas, *Tennis*, Apr. 1976

Perforated nylon uppers distinguish the adidas Nastase tennis shoes. Soft-tread sole is vulcanized to the uppers to be durable.

Basketball shoes from adidas.

adidas, *Track & Field News*, Feb. 1973

The Nastase Master tennis shoe from adidas was named after tennis pro Ilie Nastase. This ad announced the use of Cangoran® instead of kangaroo leather. The synthetic material allowed the foot to breathe like real leather, and was sprayed with an antibacterial agent to prevent infection and malodors.

The adidas SL 72, Dragon, and Country were marketed in this ad as the best shoes to wear on and off the court.

**119**

adidas, *Tennis*, Aug. 1977

adidas, *Track & Field News*, March 1979

**120**

Adidas' Marathon 80 was the company's lightest running shoe at 6.3 ounces. The heel's spoiler was designed to absorb shock and the studded sole to provide traction.

Adistar 2000 and Quicksilver by adidas.

adidas, *Track & Field News, May*

Adidas track and field shoes, the product of "relentless research and development." From top: the Apollo with nylon uppers; the rugged blue nylon Jet with ankle padding and heel wedge; and the Arrow spikeless track shoe.

adidas, *Track & Field News*, Jan. 1979

Adidas' Spider in light velour leather was designed with a half-moccasin cut to fit any foot perfectly. Was advertised as especially good on artificial tracks. Adjustable triangle elements provided custom traction control.

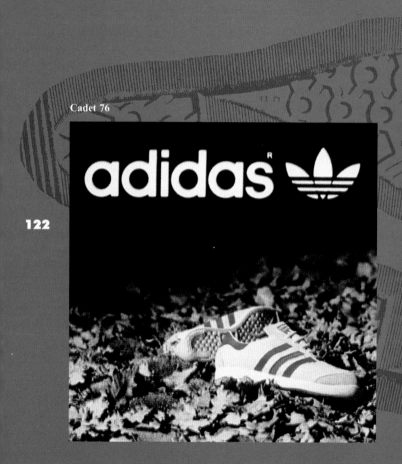

Cadet 76

122

Québec

## 1970s

**Runner**

**Another Medal Winner...**
...the adidas "Runner" shoe

adidas®

**Another Medal Winner...**
...the adidas "SL 76" training shoe

adidas®

**SL 76**

**123**

**Adistar**

**Another Medal Winner...**
...the adidas "Adistar" track shoe

adidas®

adidas, *Track & Field* News, Sep. 1976

The Tom Quaker Professional tennis shoe.

adidas, *Tennis*, July 1977

*Puma, The Athletic Journal, Sept. 1970*

TS #200 from Puma, featuring Velcro closures, four-spike soles, cowhide uppers, and extra padding at the Achilles tendon.

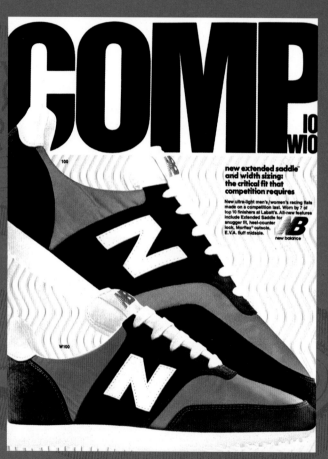

COMP
10
W10

**new extended saddle™ and width sizing: the critical fit that competition requires**

New ultra-light men's/women's racing flats made on a competition last. Worn by 7 of top 10 finishers at Labatt's. All-new features include Extended Saddle for snugger fit, heel-counter lock, Morflex® outsole, E.V.A. fluff midsole.

new balance

New Balance competition 100 and W100, an ultra light racing shoe for men and women with an extended saddle, heel-counter lock, and Morflex™ outsole.

New Balance, *Track & Field News*, Apr. 1979

Puma now makes a great leather tennis shoe.

helped us develop our new Puma tennis shoe. The end result is the finest tennis shoe a player could wear.

White top grade cowhide uppers and reinforced toe for longer wear. Specially developed one-piece cushioned rubber sole won't slip or slide on court surface. Perforated strip down the side for cooler, drier feet. Sponge insole and arch plus extra padding at the heel and ankle keep feet and legs from tiring. Available for men or women.

For a free full color catalog, write Sports Beconta.

Puma from Sports Beconta. 50 Executive Blvd., Elmsford, N.Y. 10523. Or 91 Park Lane, Brisbane, Cal. 94005

**Sports Beconta**

**PUMA**

The fine Puma leather tennis shoe.

**Puma,** *The Athletic Journal,* Sept. 1970

Hornet — This *Runner's World* 5-Star Shoe is listed as "an excellent shoe. Very good construction, excellent buy. We recommend this shoe highly." It was ranked #1 for rearfoot impact absorption.

Trainer 1980 — Given a #1 ranking for flexibility, this *Runner's* World 5-Star Shoe was called "A brand new excellent shoe. . . We recommend this shoe." It's made with soft foam replacing the insole board.

Saucony's Hornet and Trainer 1980 for men. Both running shoes were given five stars by *Runner's World Magazine.*

**Saucony/Hyde Athletic Industries,** *Track & Field News,* Jan. 1979

125

Saucony/Hyde Athletic Industries, *Track & Field News*, Aug. 1979

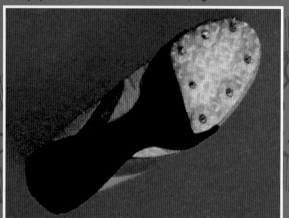

**126**

Bullet and Pacesetter by Saucony. Nylon oxford uppers with suede trim and one-piece seamless toe construction. Spikes on the nylon tap were interchangeable. The shoes were endorsed by Olympic medallist and Temple University track coach Edwin Roberts.

**J-1 NYLON WRESTLING**
WHITE WITH BLACK STRIPES
BLACK WITH WHITE STRIPES

**WRESTLING CUB**
BLACK WITH
WHITE STRIPES

WHITE WITH
BLACK STRIPES

**TIGER COMPETITION**
RED SUEDE LEATHER
WITH WHITE STRIPES

Tiger/Universal-Restlite Products, *The Athletic Journal*, Sept. 1977

Wrestling shoes from Tiger. The Gladiator in navy blue; the J-1 in white
nylon; the wrestling cub in black; and the red suede Tiger Competition.

SPARTAN B
GN33

DIG N TIGER

ATLANTIS DX
GN51

The Asics Tiger Atlantis DX
sprint shoe featured a moccasin
toe design and a nylon upper.

Asics Sports of America Inc., *Track & Field News*, Sept. 1977

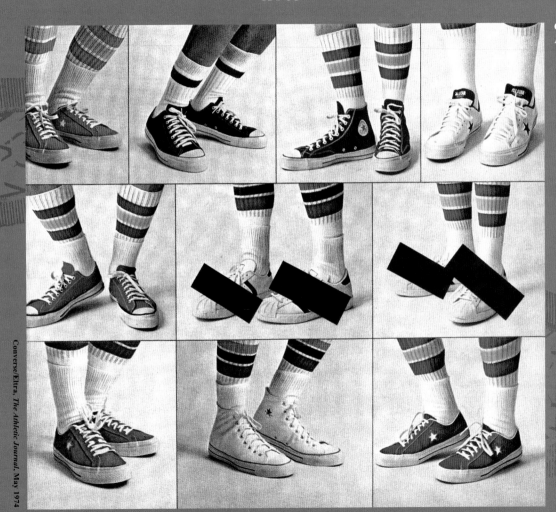

Converse
All Stars.

**130**

The 1974 tennis All Stars by Converse. Available in suede, canvas, and smooth leather uppers.

Converse/Eltra, *Tennis*, June 1974

Patented Sportwick Socks by Interwoven. Special design kept sweat away from feet in an outer layer.

Car Shown Above B210 by Datsun.

Interwoven/Kayser-Roth, *Tennis*, May 1977

Converse, *The Athletic Journal*, Oct. 1970

Converse All-Stars in canvas, leather, and suede came in seven different colors and five different styles.

131

Converse All-Stars "Chuck Taylors" in red canvas.

Converse/Eltra, *The Athletic Journal*, Sept. 1973

# 1970s

America's basketball shoe. Converse
All Stars were available in ten colors
and five styles in 1974.

Converse/Eltra, *The Athletic* Journal, Mar. 1974

Nylon and suede Converse World Class
Trainers. The wedge heel was made of re-
silient high-density materials.

132

Converse/Eltra, *Track & Field News*, May 1978

The Converse World Class Trainer in blue.

Converse's tennis shoe for women offered traction and style.

**Converse/Eltra,** *The Athletic Journal,* Dec. 1977

**Converse/Eltra,** *The Athletic Journal,* Dec. 1977

Converse basketball shoes with high tops. According to advertising, they were worn by basketball star Dr. J and most college teams.

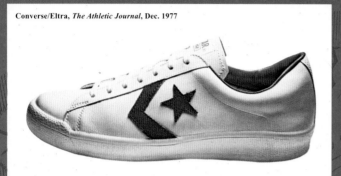

Converse/Eltra, *The Athletic Journal*, Dec. 1977

The Converse tennis shoe for men.

**134**

Nike running shoes.

The Elite (Special Marathon). Ranked #1 in Racing Flats category.

The Sting. Ranked #2 in Racing Flats.

Vainquere. Ranked #2 in Track Spikes.

Nike, *Track & Field News*, Oct. 1979

LD1000. Ranked #5 in Training Flats.

Waffle Trainer. Ranked #6 in Training Flats.

**135**

The Nike Liberator for women featured a washable foam insole that conformed to the shape of any foot.

Boston 73. Ranked #9 in Racing Flats.

Nylon Cortez. Ranked #10 in Training Flats.

Nike, *Runner's World Magazine*

Nike Triumph sprinting shoes with pyramid-patterned rear soles for extra traction. In lime with orange and blue, or electric blue with gold.

Nike, *Track & Field News*, Mar. 1978

**136**

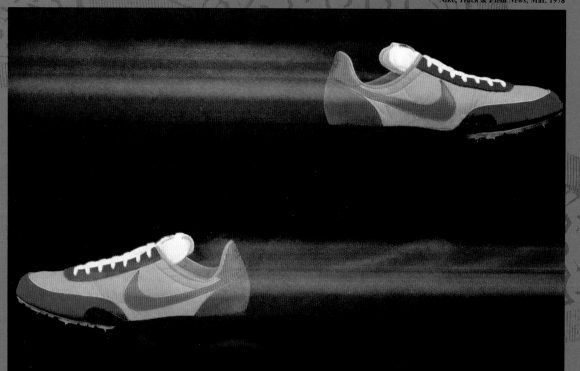

Sand-Knit, *The Athletic Journal*, May 1971

Sand-Knit, *The Athletic Journal*, Apr. 1974

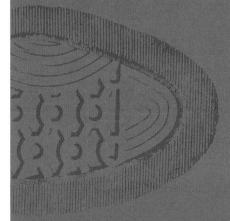

Riddell, Inc., *The Athletic Journal*, Jan. 1974

# 1980s

Superga's leather sports shoe with polyurethane sole and the company's exclusive "wrap around toe." Added style and the advantage of less toe drag.

Superga Piede Watcu Sports, *Tennis*, May 1980

140

We sell quality
by the running foot.

Foot Locker, *Runner's World Magazine*, Aug. 1980

At Foot Locker, we'll make sure you get off on the right path with the proper shoes for your particular style of running.

Whether you're into jogging, track, cross-country—or just running around, everything's right at your feet at Foot Locker.

We've got the biggest selection of the biggest names in men's and women's athletic shoes in America.

We've also got all the running accessories and clothing you'll need.

That'll save you a lot of running around to different stores—so you can spend more time running where you want. Foot Locker. The runaway favorite.

NIKE TAILWIND
NEW BALANCE 620
NIKE TEMPEST
ADIDAS LADY ORION
BROOKS RT1
ADIDAS TRX TRAINER
NIKE WAFFLE TRAINER II
NIKE DAYBREAK
SAUCONY HORNET
ETONIC BONNE BELL
ETONIC STABILIZER
NIKE LIBERATOR
SPALDING SUPER FLITE
NIKE BERMUDA
ADIDAS MARATHON 80

**foot Locker**
America's most complete athletic footwear store.

Foot Locker, *Runner's World Magazine*

**141**

WEYENBERG/stacyadams

July 1981 / RUNNER'S WORLD 99

The Action 400s by Weyenberg/Stacy Adams were inexpensive running shoes.

Spalding's The Cinch™ with a patented strap helped reduce pronation and increase efficiency.

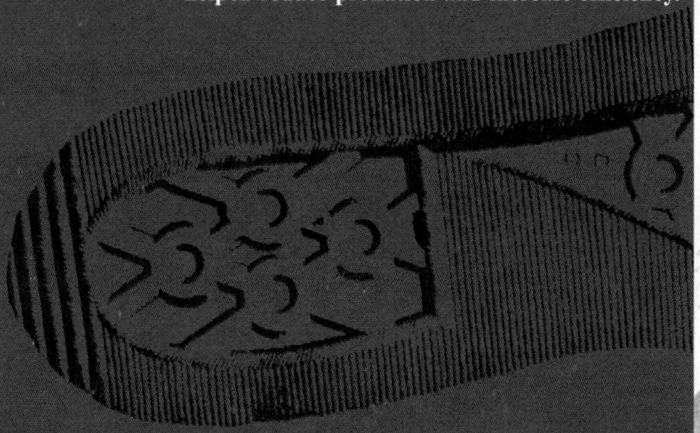

142

THE CINC

Spalding/Elite Star, *Runner's World Magazine*, Nov. 1985

Spalding, *Tennis*, July 1983

The full leather Spalding Ultra Light was advertised as the lightest tennis shoe at 10.5 ounces.

Ellesse, *Tennis*, Apr. 1984

Ellese's tennis shoes were marketed as Italian works of art and products of relentless research and design.

Spalding, *Runner's World Magazine*, Sept. 1980

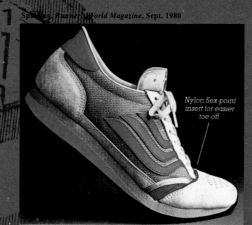

Nylon flex-point insert for easier toe-off

The Spalding Ultra Flex with nylon fabric across the ball of the shoe to add flexibility.

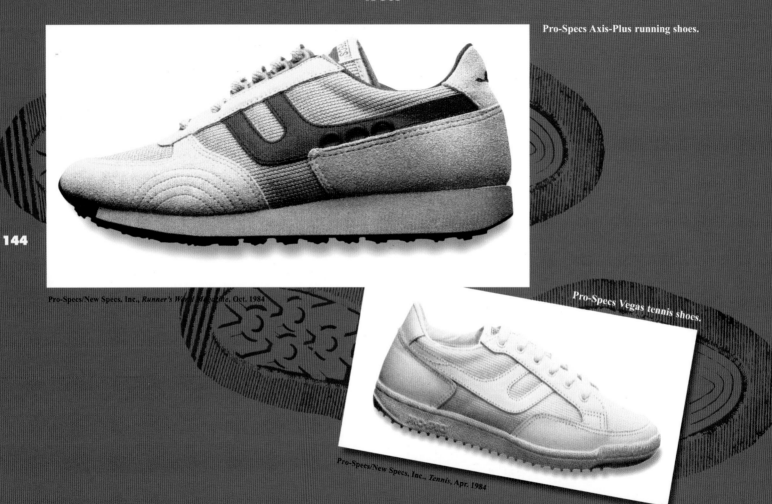

**Pro-Specs Axis-Plus running shoes.**

Pro-Specs/New Specs. Inc., *Runner's World Magazine*, Oct. 1984

**Pro-Specs Vegas tennis shoes.**

Pro-Specs/New Specs, Inc., *Tennis*, Apr. 1984

Pro-Specs, *Runner's World Magazine*, 1983 Annual

Pro-Specs/Specs International, Inc., *Runner's World Magazine*, Jan. 1980

Pro-Specs shoes were marketed as
technological products and came with
a written guarantee.

5-Star Specs Innsbruck with a thick
foam sole for lightness and shock-
absorption. Given a five-star rating by
*Runner's World* Magazine.

Ellesse Spring Collection Court Shoes for men and women.

Pre-Specs, Runner's World Magazine, Aug. 1980

The Innsbruck's "fat bottom" and the Munich II's "shock bottom," by Pro-Specs.

**Match Point by Le Coq Sportif with an extra wide outer sole.**

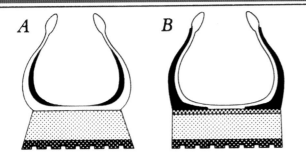

A) Conventional inside counter. B) Match Point's heel stabilizer.

Le Coq Sportif, *Tennis,* Apr. 1984

A) Conventional inside support. B) Match Point's external arch support.

Ellesse U.S.A. *Tennis,* Apr. 1986

**Ellesse Spring Collection Court Shoes for men and women.**

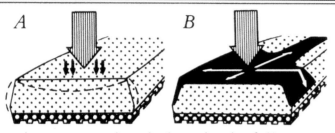

A) Traditional midsoles take the full impact directly on the heel. B) Turbotec's black high density sections disperse shock while gray low density sections absorb it.

- *Individual grooved studs contract on impact.* - *Wave-like form increases traction.*

Le Coq Sportif, *Runner's World Magazine*, 1980

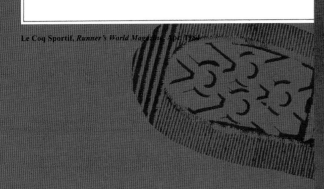

Turbotec by Le Coq Sportif featured a dual-density polyethylene sole with super shock-absorbing qualities.

Asahi tennis shoes.

Le Coq Sportif's Noah Comp court shoe, a combination of innovation and French style.

150

Asahi/Yamaha Sports Group, *Tennis*, Jan. 1981

Le Coq Sportif, *Tennis*, Apr. 1987

The Asahi PM 1 was designed with Yamaha technology to create a sole made of both natural rubber and synthetic materials.

Asahi/Yamaha Sports Group, *Tennis*, June 1983

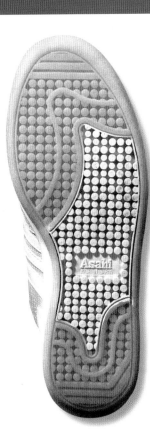

Foot-Joy, Inc., *Tennis*, Oct. 1983

Foot-Joy Tuffs for racquetball players.

Foot-Joy's Pacifica featured a dual sole that offered durability and comfort.

your competition. Instead of your feet.

Foot-Joy®

Brockton, MA 02403

**SHOES FOR ATHLETES WHO THINK.**
SEE READER SERVICE PAGE FOR MORE INFORMATION

Foot-Joy, Inc., *Tennis*, Oct. 1983

Foot-Joy Tuffs had three rows of stitching in the toe and promised durability. In nylon and suede, leather, and high-top styles.

Foot-Joy, Inc., *Tennis*, Oct. 1980

Tough tennis shoes from Head, marketed as classy off the court for casual wear.

Head, *Tennis*, Mar. 1987

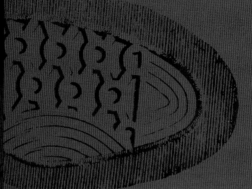

Fila Tennis shoes.

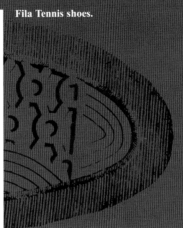

Fila, *Tennis*, Nov. 1986

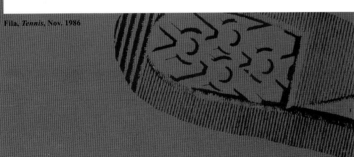

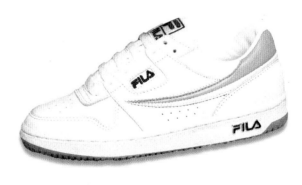

Wilson Athletic Footwear, Inc., *Tennis*, Apr. 1986

**156**

The Wilson Aggressor for men and the women's Advantage tennis shoes offered tough support and durability. In leather or double mesh.

*European flair:*

Romika promised quality craftsmanship and style in their tennis shoes.

Flash tennis shoes by Bata. The company claimed they were the first to manufacture shoes using polyurethane.

Bata, *Tennis*, Aug. 1980

The Tretorn Supra™ tennis shoe with
polyurethane sole and full length inner.

158

# IMPROVE YOUR COORDINATION

Incredible Tretorn comfort that's great for mix.
And match.

## TRETORN®
THE ULTIMATE TENNIS SHOE.

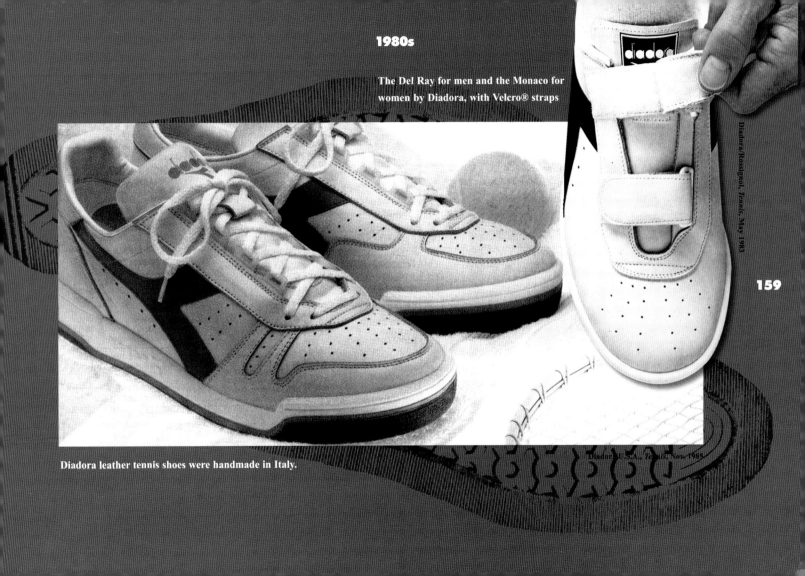

**The Del Ray for men and the Monaco for women by Diadora, with Velcro® straps**

*Diadora/Rossignol, Tennis, May 1983*

**Diadora leather tennis shoes were handmade in Italy.**

*Diadora U.S.A., Tennis, Nov 1985*

Soma's tennis shoes featured a two-part sole with a firm bottom and orthopedically molded inner.

SOMA's exclusive Duolite™ sole eliminates compromise—does the whole job with just two parts instead of many.

It's as simple as that.

*Soma-Tennis, Jan. 1981*

Autry tennis shoes with patented Actionsorb® insole, innovative tread, and CLC® system (counter lock cord) to grip the ankle.

*Autry, Tennis, Apr. 1986*

# The Lynx is loose.

The Lynx GRS1 running shoe was designed with a shock-dispersing
outsole made from dual density carbon rubber.

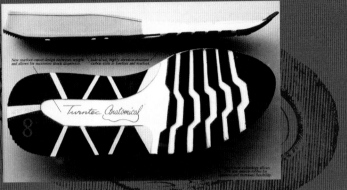

Flexlite running shoe by Turntec. Innovative outsole design to reduce use of rubber and weight of shoe.

Turntec, *Runner's World Magazine*, Mar. 1987

Turntec's running shoes featured an anatomical design that conformed to the shape of the foot to cradle it.

Turntec, *Runner's World Magazine*, Oct. 1984

Turntec, *Runner's World Magazine*, Feb. 1985

164

*Villanova, Vantage and Hugger are registered trademarks of Wolverine World Wide, Inc.

Turntec's Road Warrior.

Turntec, *Runner's World Magazine*, Nov. 1987

Turntec's Road Warrior #571 with the ZO² heel liner for extra shock-absorption.

Turntec, *Runner's World Magazine*, Sept. 1988

Turntec, *Runner's World Magazine*, Feb. 1989

Turntec running shoe.

Turntec, *Runner's World Magazine*, Aug. 1984

Roadhawk and Roadhawk Light
by Turntec. Roadhawk Light
was manufactured with polyurethane and fiberglass to create a
lightweight shoe.

Sako/California Footwear, Inc., Runner's World Magazine, Apr. 1985

**168**

Sako's work shoes were designed
with running shoe technology.

THE
SAKO SUPER

SAKO

Dealer inquiries invited!

Sako/California Footwear, Inc., Runner's World Magazine, Oct. 1984

The Sako Super™ was designed for
supinating runners to prevent extra wear
on the outside edge of the outsole.

## THE OUTSIDE STORY.
A patented super light Bar Sole designed to give you more shock absorption, more traction, a natural flex pattern, and the added bonus of more mileage.

## THE INSIDE STORY.
A super light, super cushion grooved Inner Sole with patented energy absorption zones under the heel and along the entire length of the sole.

**Pony running shoe.**

169

*Pony, Runner's World Magazine, Oct. 1980*

*Pony, Runner's World Magazine, December 1980*

The 1982 Pony running shoes featured a special patented Flexrite Bar Sole™ that offered extra flexibility.

BAREFOOT RACER

TARGA FLEX

TARGA CARRERA

FUKUOKA

PONY SPORTS & LEISURE, INC.
251 Park Avenue South, New York, N.Y. 10010

THE TRACY.

FEATS.

THE COMPLETE LINE OF PONY TENNIS SHOES IS AVAILABLE AT FINER SPORTING GOODS DEALERS AND SELECTED TENNIS PRO SHOPS.

Pony, *Tennis*, Mar. 1981

NEW COURT.

TRACY AUSTIN, ROSCOE TANNER, JOSE HIGUERAS, MEL PURCELL, PETER RENNERT, IVANA MADRUGA AND DIANNE FROMHOLTZ

ARE JUST SOME OF

FOREST HILLS.

ROSCOE TANNER

APPROACH

FOREST HILLS

# 4 ACES IN A ROW.

Pony, *Tennis*, Mar. 1984

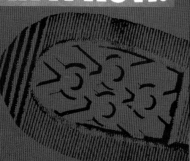

TWO SETS

TRACY AUSTIN
CENTRE COURT

## PONY

### THE MARK WITH THE CHEVRON.

VISIT YOUR AUTHORIZED PONY DEALER TO SEE
THE COMPLETE LINE OF PONY'S PERFORMANCE
ATHLETIC FOOTWEAR FOR MEN AND WOMEN.

PONY SPORTS & LEISURE, INC.
925 Paterson Plank Road, Secaucus, NJ 07094

The Gainesville and Lady
Gainesville by Pony.

Avia/Second Sole, *Runner's World Magazine*, Oct. 1986

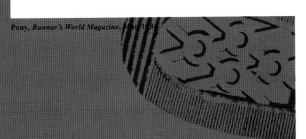

*Pony, Runner's World Magazine, March 1986*

The Avia 480 Men's Fitness featured a patented cantilever outsole and a full grain
leather upper with extended saddle.

174

Lotto tennis shoes.

**The Court**
A durable indoor court shoe with special built in support features that meet the demands of the game.

**The Runner**
A flexible lightweight running shoe that reduces muscle fatigue.

**The Competition**
A fine tuned tennis shoe that absorbs the shock and reduces the risk of ankle strain.

# BALLY
OF SWITZERLAND.

For brochure write Jerry, Bally Inc., One Bally Place, New Rochelle, NY 10801
The Competition and The Runner are also available in women's sizes.

Bally, *Runner's World Magazine*, Apr. 1983

Lotto, Newk U.S.A., *Tennis*, June 1980

**The Competition, the Runner, and the Court by Bally of Switzerland.**

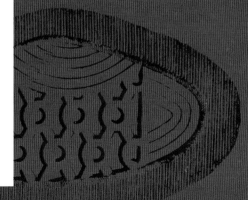

Vans Serio Style 152 running shoe was the product of years of research, testing, and planning.

Vans, *Runner's World Magazine*, May 1982

Gallenkamp Shoes, *Runner's World Magazine*

176

Jordache's running shoe featured a stabilizing heel and reflective 3M Scotchlite® trim on the heel tab and side logo. In nylon mesh with suede.

*Jordache Athletic Wear, Ltd., Runner's World Magazine, May 1982*

"Concorde" — Men's training flat
RW 5-Star

It's not just our familiar side markings which bind all Autry shoes... It's value, quality and our dedication to creating superior athletic footwear. Experience our highly rated running shoes yourself.

"Mach II" — Men's training flat
RW 4-Star

"Jet" — Men's training flat
RW 4-Star

**《《《 JETSTREAMERS**
The Action Shoes
of the 80's.

**AUTRY**
*THE ACTION PEOPLE*

"Cloud" — Women's training flat
RW 3-Star

Autry Industries, Inc., *Runner's World Magazine*, May 1980

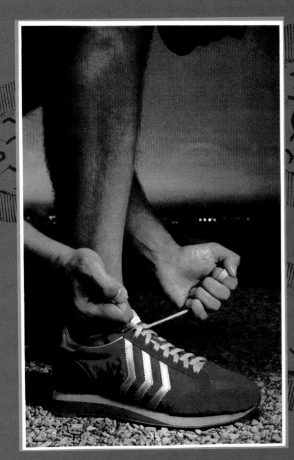

Intermark Shoe Co., *Runner's World Magazine*, Apr. 1981

The AAU LW-3103 running shoe.

Autry's Concorde running
shoe with silver accents.

Autry Industries, Inc., *Runner's World Magazine*, Dec. 1980

# How to design a winning running shoe.

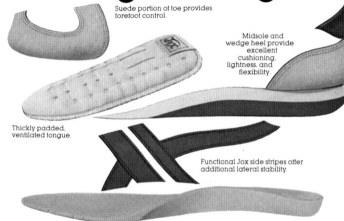

Suede portion of toe provides forefoot control.

Midsole and wedge heel provide excellent cushioning, lightness, and flexibility.

Thickly padded, ventilated tongue.

Functional Jox side stripes offer additional lateral stability.

Remarkable one-piece "trelonic" insole actually contours to the shape of your foot after running a short distance. Three layers of foam material covered in terry cloth provide cushioning and support for the exact shape of your foot.

Special layer of impregnated felt material for shock absorption and insulation.

Unique "sabre tooth" sole design gives durability and superior traction on virtually all surfaces.

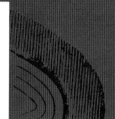

Unique "sabre tooth" sole design gives durability and superior traction on virtually all surfaces.

Weight: Men's size 9, 290 gm./10.2 oz. Women's size 7, 225 gm./7.9 oz.

## Jox Road Handlers

RW5-STAR ★★★★★ Runner's World Magazine Women's Road Handlers

RW4-STAR ★★★★ Men's Road Handlers

Jox Road Handlers® have a "trelonic" compression insole that shapes to and permanently holds the contours of your foot—a design break-through in running shoes. The "trelonic" insole combines with other special features to make Jox Road Handlers® one of the best high-performance running shoes anywhere. Men's Road Handler® $29.99. Women's Road Handler® $27.99.

Prices slightly higher in Hawaii and Puerto Rico.

*Thom McAn*

Technologically advanced running
shoes from Mizuno.

# MIZUNO

Mizuno/Colby-Bates Co., Runner's World Magazine, Jan. 1982

Russell, Runner's World Magazine, May 1980

TRX-C

**Notice the National Sports Socks by Russell. Adidas made the shoe.**

**182**

Misuno running shoes with the Mizuno Cassette Insole System, which customized to feet in six different areas, creating 81 different combinations. This special insole feature was available in the Mizuno MZ-450 and MZ-650 all-purpose trainers, and the MZ-84 racers.

# Mizuno

Marketed and distributed exclusively by Curley-Bates Co., 860 Stanton Road, Burlingame, CA 94010 (415) 697-6420

Bauer, *Runner's World Magazine*

The Bauer Eagle hard surface runner with a strap at
the top of the laces that gave a "bear hug" to feet.

adidas, *Tennis*, Apr. 1981

**The adidas Association of Tennis Professionals outdoor shoe.**

Endorsed by the ATP. Designed to meet the demands of daily tournament play, the ATP Outdoor is a supremely comfortable tennis shoe.

The vulnerable toe is reinforced to provide longer wear.

Double security: the two-tone rubber sole is cemented and stitched to the leather upper.

Start, stop and turn with ease on the multi-grip rubber sole.

**adidas**
**We've got a feeling for winning.**

The stable heel counter holds the foot firmly yet comfortably.

The Association of Tennis Professionals represents the top tennis players in the world.

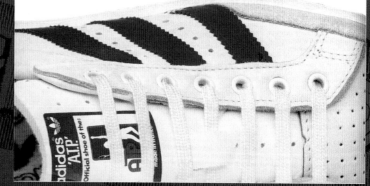

Tough, hard-wearing
STAN SMITH tennis shoe.
The leather upper is
bonded and stitched
to the durable
rubber sole.

**ATP shoes by adidas.**

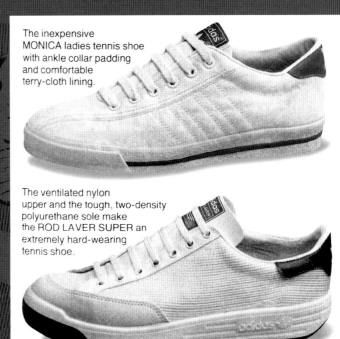

The inexpensive
MONICA ladies tennis shoe
with ankle collar padding
and comfortable
terry-cloth lining.

The ventilated nylon
upper and the tough, two-density
polyurethane sole make
the ROD LAVER SUPER an
extremely hard-wearing
tennis shoe.

adidas, tennis, Sept. 1980

Fencing    Leisure    Golf    Free-style wrestling    Indoor Sports    Long Jump

Car racing    Cross-country    Steeplechasing    Cross-country skiing    Gymnastics    Ski jumping

Shot-putting    Shooting    Marathon running    Volleyball    Javelin    Football

Greco-roman wrestling    Soccer    Baseball    Basketball    Parachuting    High Jump Straddle

Coaching    Rowing    Sprinting    Walking    Rugby    Weightlifting

Softball    Racquetball    Hiking    Cycling    Triple Jump    Training

Windsurfing    Relaxing    High Jump Flop    Boxing    Tennis    Hammer throwing

**186**

The new adidas training flat "Marathon Trainer".

The concave sole form creates excellent shock absorption.

At heel-strike the net in the mid-sole wedge distributes the shock over the entire foot area.

The adidas "Marathon Trainer" was developed to meet the needs of the serious road runner — performance and protection.

The trefoil sole profile adds to shock-absorption and provides excellent traction.

The lightweight nylon mesh upper provides optimum ventilation for the foot.

The three-part heel spoiler improves shock absorption even on uneven surfaces.

**adidas**
We've got a feeling for winning.

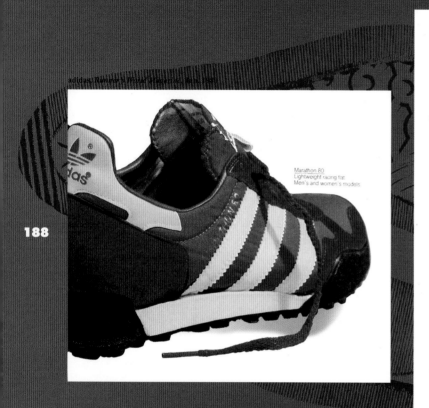

adidas: Runner's World Magazine, April 1981

Marathon 80
Lightweight racing flat.
Men's and women's models.

TRX Trainer
All-round training flat.
Men's and women's models.

Marathon Trainer
Competition training flat.
Men's and women's models.

adidas ®

The adidas Galaxy racing flat with sole designed for running on roads and perforated uppers for maximum ventilation.

adidas, *Runner's World Magazine*, June 1981

The adidas Boston training shoe with a terry covered inlay, lots of padding, and tricot lining at the heel.

Introducing the adi-STAR® 80, the newest development in track shoes, incorporating the latest technological advances.

Spike constellation can be varied to suit individual needs and conditions.

The foot-form heel ensures excellent fit and support.

The adi-STAR® 80 features screw-in conical spikes, which optimise the 'catapult' effect of synthetic tracks.

The adi-STAR® 80 with lightweight nylon uppers weighs only $3\frac{1}{2}$ oz*.

The up-swept sole with hard plastic nubs ensures no slipping in the curve.

The adi-STAR® 80 with lightweight nylon uppers weighs only 3¹/₂ oz*.

The up-swept sole with hard plastic nubs ensures no slipping in the curve.

*Men's size 8¹/₂.

**adidas** We've got a feeling for winning.

The adi-STAR® sprint shoe.

support your running habit

PRODUCT:
Silverstar.™
FUNCTION:
Training shoe.
BENEFIT:
Light weight with excellent shock absorption.
CUSHIONING:
Two-density polyurethane midsole with a unique inlay sole system for

The adidas Silverstar training shoe.

Puma tennis shoe.

What Martina ties up before she ties up the competition.

When Martina arrives on court she's wearing high performance tennis shoes from Puma. She's also wearing her exclusive Advantage line of colorful, comfortable Puma apparel.
Try donning our clothes and tying on our MN Pro tennis shoes for your next match. Then like Martina, watch your cross court rivals unravel.

PUMA
Our word for quality.

*Puma, Tennis, Apr. 1986*

This Puma shoe was named after Tennis Hall of Famer Guillermo Vilas.

**Seventeen-year-old Boris Becker won Wimbledon wearing a pair of puma tennis shoes.**

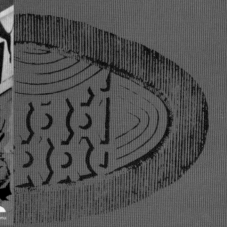

*Puma, Tennis, July 1980*

Puma, *Track & Field News*, Oct. 1981

The Skeets track shoe by Puma featured a curved heel for support and stability.

Fast Rider

Lite Rider

Track Rider

The angled, conical studs of the new Puma Federbein sole spread on impact to give maximum traction, stability and cushioning, even on the roughest of terrain.

**PUMA**

Puma, *Runner's World* Magazine, Nov. 1980

**Puma's Fast Rider, Light Rider, and Track Rider featured the Federbein sole with v-shaped studs for extra traction.**

Puma's R System Computerized shoe featured a computer chip in the heel of the shoe that recorded the time, distance, and calories burnt during a run. The electronic device plugged into Apple IIE, Commodore 64 or 128, or IBM PC computers.

# Whisper

There's nothing hush hush about the way these high performance satin and suede "Whispers" have caught fire with women runners.

The Whisper's last is designed exclusively for women to provide superior fit and torsional stability, while the double heel counter offers an extra measure of stability to inhibit over pronation.

And Whisper's PE wedge is a superior shock absorber, designed to cushion the blows of footstrike from heel to toe. A removable footbed with unique collapsible pressure ridges at the heel and a flexible forefoot offers added cushioning and comfort.

In five shimmering color selections, Whisper is a perfect way to improve your running style.

Exercise your right to choose performance in the shade that's fitting for you.

PUMA

*Puma, Runner's World Magazine, Nov. 1985*

The Elite Rider training shoe from Puma with a stabilizing "orthotic footbed," a semi-rigid insert that cupped the heel and ran along almost the entire length of the shoe.

PUMA is quality ...denn macht's mit Qualität PUMA

*Puma, Runner's World Magazine*

Puma's Strider was designed to absorb shock along the heel and outside edge of the foot, where studies showed the most impact occurred during running. The sole of the shoe was made from highly carbonized rubber to withstand miles of road wear.

Puma, *Runner's World Magazine*, Apr. 1983

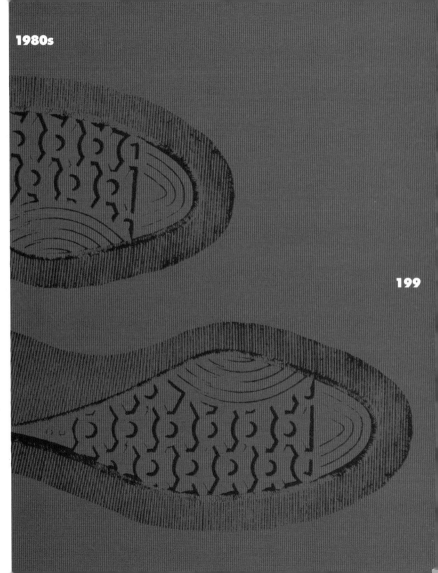

The Reliant LX from Puma was a road shoe, designed to withstand the wear of the road and protect the foot. Mesh uppers were reinforced by suede and leather.

The Lab-1 by Puma.

200

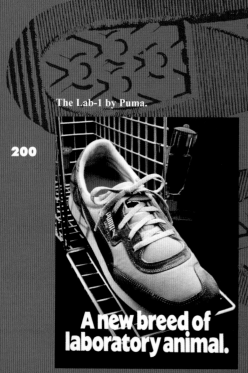

# A new breed of laboratory animal.

Puma, *Runner's World Magazine*, Feb. 1983

# It puts the pavement at a disadvantage.

Puma, *Runner's World Magazine*, Apr. 1987

Puma, *Runner's World Magazine*, Oct. 1983.

The RLX from Puma featured a high density molded External Heel Stabilizer that stretched high into the heel area along the medial, or inner, side of the foot. Advertised as a tough shoe that offered arch support, shock absorption, and stability.

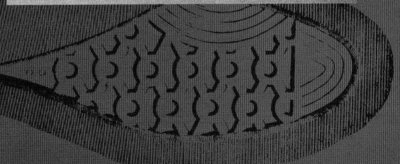

201

Puma's SAAS1 featured a unique, patented sole designed to provide shock absorption and stability. V-shaped studs were made from carbonized rubber for durability. The rigid heel counter was extended on the inner heel for greater stability.

202

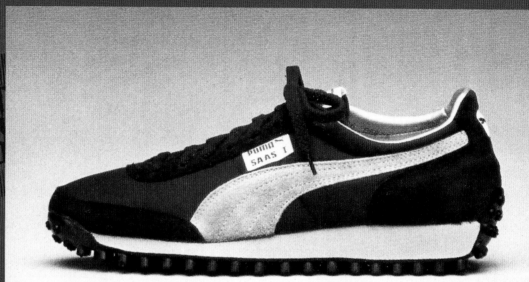

Puma, *Runner's World Magazine*, Oct. 1981

ATLETICA ITALIA

Broaden your base with Lotto Italia's exclusive system of *Wide Cleat Placement* for superior *heel stability*.

These soccer cleats from Lotto Italia were specially designed with wide cleat placement for extra stability.

**GULLIT PRO** Sizes 3-13
All "NAPPA" leather upper. 14 stud stitched rubber outsole.
Extended leather tongue that folds over.

**MAURO PRO** Sizes 3-13
"NAPPA" leather vamp and 14 stud stitched rubber outsole.

*lotto* ITALIA

Lotto Itlaia, *Soccer*, May-June 1989

Mitre soccer cleats.

Mitre, *Soccer*, May-June 1987

**1980s**

**Mitre soccer cleats.**

**Mitre's TATU Signature Series®.**

Hot looks in an all-leather upper that is available in three different soles:

Milan (shown): Molded cleat for semi-soft fields.

Madrid: Replaceable cleats for soft, wet or muddy fields.

Dominator: Unique cleats and sole configuration for hard ground play.

Mitre, *Soccer*, May-June 1987

**204**

786tr
Hard ground

786m
Grass

786i
Hardwood/
synthetic

# Saucony®

Shoes for the
great American athlete.

205

Saucony 786 Series shoes.

Saucony/Athletic Industries, *Soccer*, July-Aug. 1987
A division of Hyde Athletic Industries, Centennial Industrial Park, Peabody, MA 01961

Nike's Euromatch soccer shoes were advertised as the most expensive soccer shoe that Nike ever made. Detachable polyurethane cleats, twin-layer nylon sole plates, calfskin uppers were some of the shoe's features.

ABC Sports Adams-Mills Hosiery Co.
*Runner's World Magazine*, Apr. 1980

206

These ABC sports socks provided extra protection to athletes with their absorbent lining, knit-in heel, and ankle and arch support.

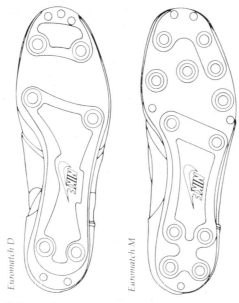

Euromatch D

Euromatch M

Underneath that leather is a nylon vamp lining to make sure the shoe holds its shape. Followed by pigskin, for a fit as soft as it is supple.

When things dry out, there's the Euromatch M. With twice as many molded cleats—angled, beveled and graduated in length with shorter cleats in front to reduce foot drag.

There's no question about the Euromatch's superiority. Before we marketed it here in the states, we took it on tour with European pros, where it received rave reviews.

There's just one little problem. This is a competition shoe. But after a couple of grueling matches, you may be tempted to wear it to practice. Don't. It can be an expensive habit to kick.

**NIKE**

Beaverton, Oregon

*Nike, Soccer, July-Aug. 1985*

Sock Racer

Spiridon Gold

Axis

Pursuit

Air Edge

Vendetta T/C

**NIKE**
Beaverton, Oregon

Nike, *Runner's World Magazine,* Fall 1986

Nike's Challenge Court shoes with an extended
ankle collar were suitable for various sports.

The bi-level hobnail cupsole provides excellent traction. And
with a nylon mesh upper, the shoe
is extremely lightweight. It even
accepts custom orthotics.
    So if you have a difficult
time restricting your feet to a
single sport, slip them into the
Challenge
Court.
They'll be
devoted.

**NIKE**
Beaverton, Oregon

TENNIS/May 1983  99

SEE READER SERVICE PAGE FOR MORE INFORMATION

Nike, *Tennis,* May 1983

Nike Air Ace featured the revolutionary Nike-Air™ midsole with cushioning and shock-absorbing qualities.

*NIKE-Air™ midsole*

The Nike Dasher, an indoor soccer shoe in non-stretch Oxford nylon for a lighter, more durable shoe. The cup sole offered lateral stability for sudden pivots and stops. In grey and maroon, blue and white, and black and silver.

*Lighter weight: approx. 363 grams in size 9.*

*Shaved arch area for a snug fit.*

*Cupsole for greater lateral stability.*

*PVC heel counter to help lock foot in place.*

*Non-stretch Oxford nylon for longer life.*

*Flex-grooves for improved flexibility.*

*Suede toe foxing for better bond to outsole.*

The Dasher.

*Nike, Soccer May-June 1985*

The Nike Air V-series for women included the Vector, the Vengeance, and the Vortex.

The Nike Air Stab for women was advertised as a lightweight and flexible shoe that offered stability and cushioning.

Nike, *Runner's World Magazine*, Oct. 1985

Nike, *Runner's World Magazine*, Dec. 1988

Tempest, the Air-Sole™ for women.

**The Tempest running shoe by Nike.**

Nike, Runner's World Magazine, Feb, 1980.

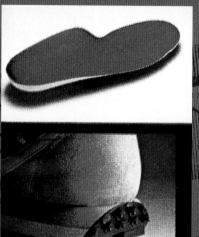

The Nike Liberator for women featured a PermaFoam insole that molded to the shape of the foot and a WAFFLE outsole for traction.

212

Nike, *Runner's World Magazine*, May 1980

*Nike Duellist. Extremely lightweight Phylon™ cushioning.*

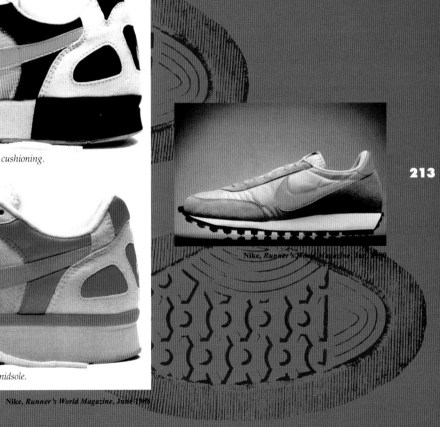

*Nike, Runner's World Magazine, Jan.*

*Nike Air Mariah. Full length Nike-Air® midsole.*

*Nike, Runner's World Magazine, June 1988.*

Nike running shoe.

The Nike Pegasus was an affordable running shoe with Nike Air technology. A waffle outsole and flared heel add traction and stability.

214

*Nike, Runner's World Magazine*

*Nike, Track & Field News, Jan. 1982*

**The Odyssey from Nike.**

*The Odyssey*

Nike, Track & Field news, Febr 1983

Nike, *Runner's World Magazine*, Sept. 1986

The Nike Sock Racer in yellow.

The Nike Sock Trainer featured a contoured foot bed
to provide support to the arch, heel, and forefoot.
The nylon mesh upper stretched to fit any foot.

Nike, *Runner's World Magazine*, Oct. 1985

Zoom Ultra

Zoom Light

Zoom Ultra

*Nike-Air cushioning and support.*

Zoom Light

*A light sprint shoe that fits like a glove.*

Internationalist

*It's versatile and lightweight.*

Rival Plus

*For red teams.*

High Jump '88

*Featuring a forefoot EVA take-off pad.*

Long Jump '88

*A unique midsole enhances takeoff leverage.*

Rival Plus

*For blue teams.*

Javelin '88

*With a full-length ten spike nylon plate.*

Shot And Discus '88

*For training or competition.*

Rival Plus

*For teams that aren't red and blue.*

**Track shoes from Nike.**

Nike, *Runner's World Magazine*, Feb. 1989

*For distance running . . .*
Zoom D

*For cross country . . .*
Zoom X

*For all purpose running . . .*
Zoom I

*For the pole vault . . .*
PV 19

*For all purpose running . . .*
Flame

*For the shot, discus . . .*
SD 73

*For the long jump . . .*
LJ II

*For the high jump . . .*
HJ 8

*For the javelin . . .*
J 300

*For the triple jump . . .*
TJ 60

**NIKE**
*Beaverton, Oregon*

**More track shoes from Nike.**

Nike, *Track & Field News*, 1984

Nike's Aurora running flat for women featured a full-length Nike-Air™ midsole.

218

The Nike Waffle Trainers were built on the same lasts as their Zoom series track shoe with spikes. The outsole's waffles provide traction in addition to shock absorption.

Nike's Terra Trainer was marketed as a lightweight shoe with a Phylon™ midsole.

*Terra Trainer*

*Women's Terra Trainer*

Nike Air Max for women and men.

Nike's Air Max Light for women and men.

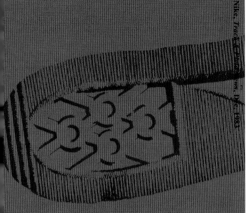

*Women's Air Max*

*Men's Air Max*

*Women's Air Max Light*

*Men's Air Max Light*

Nike, *Track & Field News*, Mar. 1987

Nike, *Runner's World Magazine*, Feb. 1989

The Nike Air Sock was lightweight and featured a stretch mesh forefoot upper for an almost customized fit.

220

Nike, *Runner's World Magazine* May 1981

Triumph

Vainqueur

Fly

Universe

Sprint Sister

Nike racing flats.

Nike, *Runner's World Magazine*, June 1980

EAGLE

AURORA

LIBERATOR

TEMPEST

EQUATOR

BERMUDA

TAILWIND

YANKEE LADY

MARIAH

MAGNUM

COLUMBIA

ATLANTA

DAYBREAK

CENTURION

LDV

BOSTON

YANKEE

WAFFLE R

INTERNATIONALIST

*Nike, Track & Field News, Oct. 1980*

**The Nike Running Line was composed of shoes that were designed for particular types of runners with distinct foot characteristics.**

The Etonic Catalyst tennis shoe was designed to move with the foot and increase mobility. The absence of a heel lift was meant to give greater control.

222

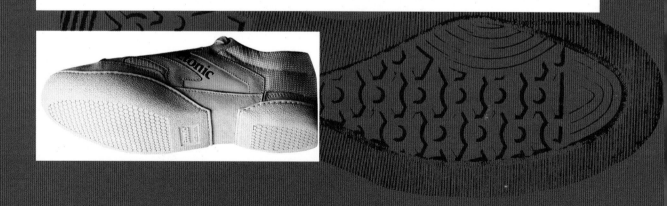

The Etonic Allegro™ was designed with a contoured heel to better accommodate the way a runner's foot hits the ground. The outsole was designed to offer optimized traction while keeping the shoe lightweight. The shoe was sold with a money-back guarantee that it would improve performance.

Etonic, *Runner's World Magazine*, Aug. 1983

Etonic's Alpha 1 featured the Dynamic Reaction Plate.™ This fiberglass insert was supposed to increase stability by limiting foot motion and heel penetration, and provide a springboard effect by thrusting the foot forward.

Etonic, *Runner's World Magazine*, Aug. 1982

Etonic's Eclipse Racer (left) and Trainer (right) were anatomically designed to provide a better fit. They also feature a dual rubber sole with two types of tread for cushioning and durability.

Etonic, *Runner's World Magazine*, Feb. 1981

The Etonic Courier running shoe offered extra support and the patented Etonic rear-foot lacing system.

Etonic, *Runner's World Magazine*, Apr. 1982

Etonic's Eclipse racing flat.

Epsilon

Allegro

Starion

Etonic, Runner's World Magazine, Mar. 1980

226

The Roadworker by Etonic.

Etonic running shoes.

*Vega*

*Women's Stabilizer*

*Quasar*

Etonic, *Runner's World Magazine*, Mar. 1984

Etonic, *Runner's World Magazine*, Aug. 1980

**Running shoes from Reebok.**

These are the world's finest running shoes. They are the culmination of seventy-five years of specialization by the Reebok family of Britain. The ratings prove it; the records prove it; you can prove it too. No matter what your running requirements are.

**＊Inca W**
The distance spike for 400 meters and up. A record holder for European cross country events.

**＊World Ten**
Designed and engineered for 10,000 meter and marathon perfection. A long-standing international record holder.

**Shadow I/Shadow III**
The competitor's training shoe for men and women. A combination of ten key features separate this shoe from all others.

**＊Fab-XC**
Designed exclusively for Orienteering. It presently holds many key English and European titles.

**10K**
A specialty shoe for 5 kilometer and 10 kilometer road racing. Also, a superior indoor track shoe.

**＊Midas**
A racing flat track lasted for close fit. Honeycombed rolled-edge sole for greater speed and comfort.

**Aztec and Aztec Princess**
Our most popular training and distance racing shoes for men and women.

＊Not presently available through U.S. retail outlets. Inquiries welcomed.

*Reebok, Runner's World Maga*

Reebok's Ex-O-Fit was advertised as the first fitness shoe of the '80s, ideal for indoor workouts. Made of garment leather in white, beige, and black.

Reebok U.S.A., June 1984

The Act 600 tennis shoe by Reebok
included a pre-molded PVC heel
counter for stability and motion control.

The Phase 1 by Reebok featured a
multi-layered sole and "technically
advanced cushioning."

Reebok, *Tennis*, Nov. 1985

*Tennis*, Dec. 1983

**230**

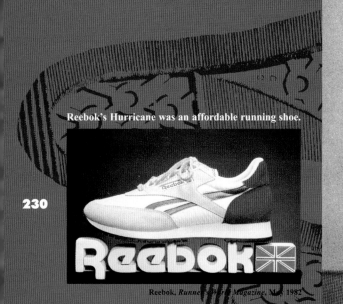

Reebok's Hurricane was an affordable running shoe.

Reebok, *Runner's World Magazine*, May 1982

# VICTORY XL...
## PERFORMANCE PLUS

Everybody likes the look of Reebok's Victory XL. But, it's the serious runner who appreciates the inner beauty of its high performance construction. From the cooling 600-denier mesh toe to the pronation protection of the Foster Heel Cradle,™ the Victory XL's built for comfort and running safety. Run to your Reebok dealer. Get the whole inside story. You'll agree, Victory XL is Performance Plus!

Reebok, *Runner's World Magazine*, May 1982

The Reebok TD was designed to prevent pronation and offer maximum stability to the foot with a complex seven-part system.

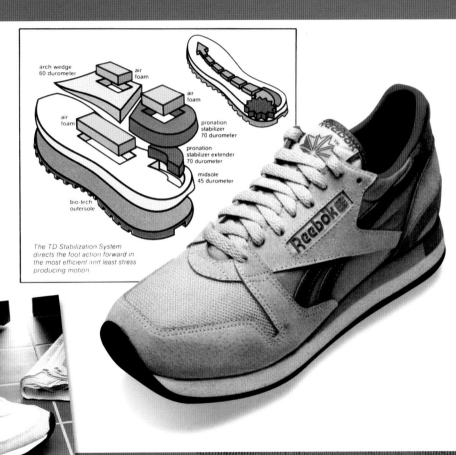

arch wedge
60 durometer

air
foam

air
foam

air
foam

pronation
stabilizer
70 durometer

pronation
stabilizer extender
70 durometer

midsole
45 durometer

bio-tech
outersole

The TD Stabilization System directs the foot action forward in the most efficient and least stress producing motion.

With a Gore-Tex® inner liner, the Reebok Victory G was marketed as a "foul weather running shoe."

Reebok, *Runner's World Magazine*, Oct. 1981

Reebok, *Runner's World Magazine*, Aug. 1983

**The Sydney Maree Trainer by Reebok.**

**The Spitfire by Reebok, a lightweight, flat-soled running shoe with EVA midsole and heel wedge.**

**232**

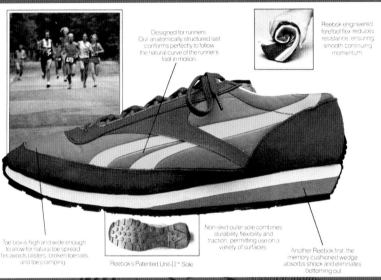

Designed for runners.
Our anatomically structured last
conforms perfectly to follow
the natural curve of the runner's
foot in motion.

Reebok engineered
forefoot flex reduces
resistance, ensuring
smooth continuing
momentum.

Toe box is high and wide enough
to allow for natural toe spread.
This avoids blisters, broken toenails,
and toe cramping.

Reebok's Patented Unit-II™ Sole

Non-skid outer sole combines
durability, flexibility and
traction, permitting use on a
variety of surfaces.

Another Reebok first, the
memory cushioned wedge
absorbs shock and eliminates
bottoming out.

Reebok. *Runner's World Magazine*, Oct. 1980

**These expensive Reebok Aztec Princesses retailed at sixty
American dollars in 1980 when this ad was published.**

**Asics sneakers and sports apparel.**

Asics. *Runner's World Magazine*

The Asics GEL Epirus featured a GEL pad filled with a semi-viscous silicon gel in the forefoot and rearfoot to absorb shock.

234

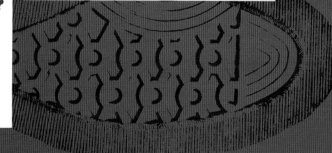

Asics, *Runner's World Magazine*

**Tiger's Alliance by Asics featured a two-layer rippled midsole designed to absorb and deflect shock, and give a spring-like effect.**

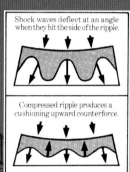

Shock waves deflect at an angle when they hit the side of the ripple.

Compressed ripple produces a cushioning upward counterforce.

235

*Asics Tiger Corp., Running World Magazine, Sept. 1984*

**GT II running shoes from Asics featured GEL in the midsoles.**

**The Striker ST™ by Asics included the Wingfoot XL™ heel insert, made from Goodyear Tire and Rubber Company.**

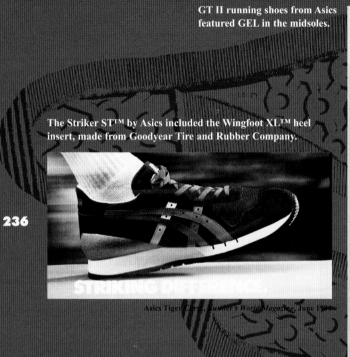

STRIKING DIFFERENCE.

Asics Tiger, *The Runner's World Magazine*, June 1985

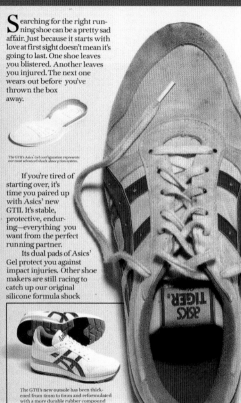

Searching for the right running shoe can be a pretty sad affair. Just because it starts with love at first sight doesn't mean it's going to last. One shoe leaves you blistered. Another leaves you injured. The next one wears out before you've thrown the box away.

The GTII's Asics' Gel configuration represents our most advanced shock absorption system.

If you're tired of starting over, it's time you paired up with Asics' new GTII. It's stable, protective, enduring—everything you want from the perfect running partner.

Its dual pads of Asics' Gel protect you against impact injuries. Other shoe makers are still racing to catch up our original silicone formula shock absorber that works better and lasts longer than traditional cushioning systems.

Asics' Gel also allows the GTII to maintain its superior stability—biomechanical tests indicate the GTII is 21% more stable than the top-of-the-line "air" shoe. And the integrated heel pillar and heel counter comfortably control motion.

Built to last, the GTII's Ecsaine upper and improved carbon rubber heel outsole ruggedly withstand miles of trials and tribulations.

A high-density midsole pillar delivers great strides in motion control.

The GTII's new outsole has been thickened from 4mm to 6mm and reformulated with a more durable rubber compound that lasts longer, even under the heaviest heel strikes.

You're going to give your next pair of running shoes some of the best miles of your life. We've made the GTII worthy of such devotion. See what we mean by calling 1-800-447-4700 today for the name of the Asics Tiger dealer nearest you.

**asics®**
THE CHOICE OF FANATICS

Asics, *Runner's World Magazine*, Dec. 1988

The Asics Tiger X-BR and
Pan Am running shoes.

The Asics Tiger X-Caliber for men and women.

LADY X-CALIBER/X-CALIBER

*Asics Tiger, Runner's World Magazine,* Jan. 1980

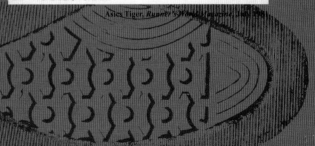

The Asics Tiger RX was designed with a wider, deeper shape to promote natural biomechanical function. The shoe was supposed to maintain stability and flexibility.

**238**

The Saucony Ultimate tennis shoe.

# BY PRESCRIPTION ONLY.

Asics Tiger Corp., *Track & Field News*, July 1984

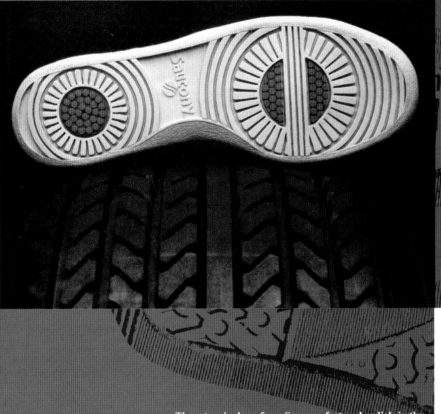

These tennis shoes from Saucony featured radials in the outsoles to assist with pivots, turns, and sudden stops.

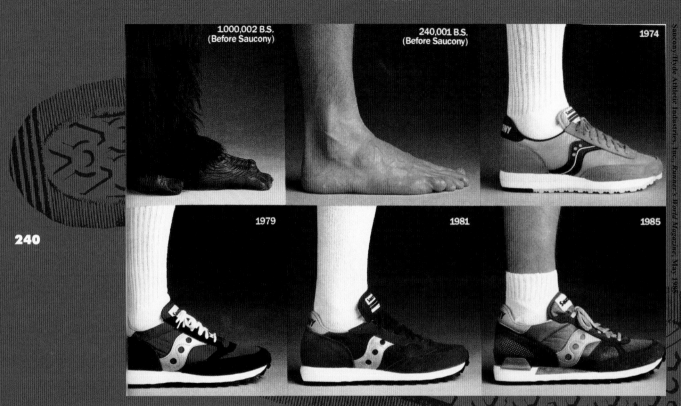

1,000,002 B.S.
(Before Saucony)

240,001 B.S.
(Before Saucony)

1974

1979

1981

1985

Saucony/Hyde Athletic Industries, Inc. *Runner's World Magazine*, May 1985.

The Shadow by Saucony evolved from the company's Jazz and Freedom Trainer. Reinforced rubber around the Shadow's outsole added extra cushioning and support, while a motion controller and shank insert in the midsole were included for stability. The heel was covered with reflective tape and a protective screen for night visibility.

Saucony/Hyde Athletic Industries, Inc. *Runner's World Magazine*, Jan. 1985

The Americas by Saucony were designed with durable and breathable mesh uppers, studded outsoles made of carbonized rubber, and a soft plastic pad for cushioning and stability.

Saucony Jazz featured "Butterfly Bal lacing" to better fit wide and narrow feet, a triangular outsole stud pattern, and a removable, machine-washable sock liner.

242

Saucony/Hyde Athletic Industries, Inc., *Runner's World Magazine*, Oct. 1982

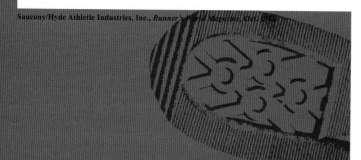

Saucony's Freedom Trainer featured an exclusive compression plug in the midsole to increase stability and prevent pronation.

Saucony/Hyde Athletic Industries, Inc., *Runner's World Magazine*, Oct. 1981

Saucony's Flite running shoe with mesh and pig-skin uppers featured an "Indy 500" carbon rubber outsole with bar tread on the heel and triangular studs on the forefoot.

Saucony/Hyde Athletic Industries, Inc., *Runner's World Magazine*, May 1984

**243**

Saucony/Hyde Athletic Industries, Inc., *Runner's World Magazine*, July 1982

The Dixon by Saucony was developed with the help of runner Rob Dixon. A special rearfoot plastic insert, called the "Dutch-man," was included to absorb shock and control pronation. The horseshoe-shaped insert was placed between the midsole and the upper. The outsole's tread featured horizontally placed bars, and the heel was reinforced and square-shaped.

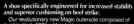

Saucony's Magic featured an innovative tread design and lacing system. The Magic's removable sock insert contained the Wingfoot™ XL heel strike cushion, a lightweight rubber insert supposed to protect the heel by distributing shock evenly.

Saucony/Hyde Athletic Industries, Inc., *Runner's World Magazine*, Apr. 1981

Saucony's Freedom was a lightweight running shoe that featured a reinforcing strip in the forefoot area. Pigskin reinforced the mesh uppers in stress areas.

New Balance, *Tennis*, Mar. 1981

new balance **NB**

**CT**

The New Balance CT tennis shoe featured ballistic mesh uppers reinforced with foam and tricot. Leather across the saddle and toe of the shoe was included for motion control and stress reduction, and a foam insert for comfort.

New Balance, *Track & Fields News*, Aug. 1981

The lightweight Comp 200 was part of New Balance's Comp Series.

New Balance competition running shoes were advertised as technologically advanced and featured curved lasts to mimic the natural shape of the foot.

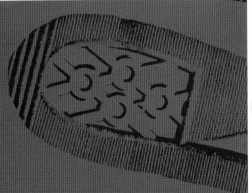

New Balance, *Track & Field News*, Aug. 1983

The New Balance 390 was advertised as a versatile running shoe for use on roads or trails. The 200 denier nylon vamp was combined with a swaybar toe piece, shank support, studded outsole, and a 60-weight Surlyn counter.

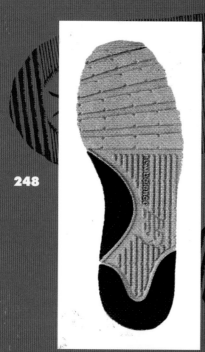

**248**

new balance **B**

**390**

New Balance, Runner's World Magazine, Oct. 198

The New Balance 410 was marketed as a shoe for new runners. It included some of the basic features of the company's more sophisticated shoes, like an extended saddle and an extended medial counter. The 410 was an adaptation of the New Balance 420.

New Balance, *Runner's World Magazine*

The New Balance 420.

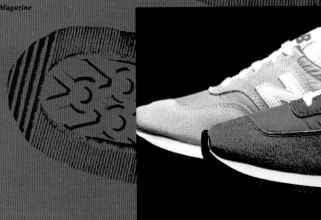

New Balance/The Athletic Attic, *Runner's World Magazine*

The New Balance 555 was designed to be a super durable shoe, with a carbon rubber houndstooth outsole that released any turf picked up during impact. The forefoot of the shoe was slip-lasted, while the rearfoot was conventionally lasted to provide more control.

The New Balance 455.

New Balance, *Runner's World Magazine*

New Balance, *Runner's World Magazine*

The New Balance 730 was designed to almost completely eliminate medial and lateral stress with a sole made from three different materials. The shoe's double-density counter was created by laminating a second counter material over the polyethylene Stanbee counter, then heating the combination and molding it to the precise width of the shoe. This feature was supposed to increase stability.

The New Balance 660, a lightweight trainer with flexible outsole, super protective and shock absorbing midsole, and a pre-molded counter in the heel, evolved from the New Balance 620.

New Balance's 770 soft running shoe utilized a midsole wedge made from *Nubalite*, which added bounce and cushioning to the shoe. A horseshoe insert in the heel provided stability, and carbon rubber plugs in the outsole were included to reduce wear and rollover.

New Balance, *Runner's World* Magazine, July 1988

The men's Phaeton™ and women's Selena™ running shoes from Converse were marketed as shoes that could reduce knee injuries. A rearfoot stabilizer was included to reduce overpronation, removable insoles molded to feet, and a slip lasted construction provided extra flexibility.

Converse, Runner's World, December 01, 1981

9B

9D

9EE

9EEEE

The New Balance M476. Like other New Balances, these athletic shoes came in a variety of sizes and widths for a better fit.

# TOO WILD?

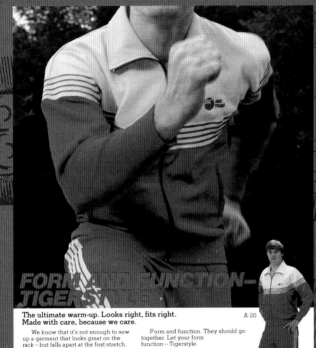

**The ultimate warm-up. Looks right, fits right.**
**Made with care, because we care.**

A-20

We know that it's not enough to sew up a garment that looks great on the rack—but falls apart at the first stretch.

Look at the inside of the Tiger warm-up. No messy loose threads. Straight stitching. Pockets that don't flop around. Little details make big garments. And fabrics that hold up—wash after wash.

Check the style above. Our model A-20, typically Tiger: athletic function with stylish form. The unique four-stripe cape shoulder with coordinated stripe in pants in six color combinations. Ask for it at your favorite specialty shop, sports or department store.

Form and function. They should go together. Let your form function—Tigerstyle.

**ASICS TIGER**
**SPORT WEAR**
ASICS Sports of America, Inc.

2052 ALTON AVENUE.
IRVINE, CALIFORNIA 92714, U.S.A

*JELENK has been replaced by ASICS TIGER.